RANT

The true story of one individual's campaign against the big banks in an attempt to save the world's economy

by M. K. Hoffman

Copyright © 2021, M. K. Hoffman

All rights reserved. Printed in the U.S.A.

No part of this publication may be reproduced or transmitted in any form or by any means, electronic or mechanical, including photocopy, recording or any information storage and retrieval system now known or to be invented, without permission in writing from the publisher, except by a reviewer who wishes to quote brief passages in connection with a review written for inclusion in a magazine, newspaper or broadcast.

Quantity Purchases:
Companies, professional groups, clubs, and other organizations may qualify for special terms when ordering quantities of this title.
For information, email info@ebooks2go.net,
or call (847) 598-1150 ext. 4141.
www.ebooks2go.net

Published in the United States by eBooks2go, Inc.
1827 Walden Office Square, Suite 260, Schaumburg, IL 60173

ISBN: 978-1-5457-5422-1

Library of Congress Cataloging in Publication

This book is dedicated to my parents,
Allan and Harriet, who instilled in me the concept
of doing the right thing.

Acknowledgement

I would like to thank some of those who contributed to this book through their ideas, comments, encouragement, guidance and inspiration:

Margo Golov, Andrew Golov, Pat Augustine, Ted Solomon, Rocco Saragusa, Mark Harrington, Janet Cromley, and Elyse Trevers.

Foreword

In the modality of the times, everyone wants to pass the buck and then pass judgment on the other guy; to sit back suffering, complaining and acting like there is nothing to be done. It is so rampant that businesses use this to bilk us out of trillions of dollars.

The mighty Roman Empire did not fall because they were defeated in battle. They fell because corruption was rampant and accountability was all but non-existent. We are headed down the same path, Fortunately for us, there are still people like Marc Hoffman who are paying attention and doing what they can to hold others accountable.

He is not a hero. He is just a responsible citizen doing what all responsible citizens should do. I found this book charming, witty and inspiring. Let's hope he inspires the next wave of responsible citizens before we begin to write the downfall of the American Empire.

Author's Note

I have recently come across a quote translated from Dante Alighieri's Divine Comedy written in the early 1300's. It related to my experiences so closely that I had to include it. It goes as follows:

"The darkest places in hell are reserved for those who maintain their neutrality during times of moral crisis."

This tells me three things. Apparently, over the last 700 years, styles have changed drastically. We do not dress the way we did seven hundred years ago. Technology has changed a thousand times over if not a million times, but people have not changed at all.

It must be getting very crowded down there in the dark.

"An interesting, funny, tragic snapshot of a troubling course of events, made readable by the author's clear, incisive, witty lens." – Newsday

The following pages reflect the experiences, opinions, recollections, reasoning and conclusions of the author. Some may agree and some may not. Some names have been changed to protect the not so innocent.

Chapter 1

Hurricane Katrina crossed southern Florida on the morning of Thursday, August 25th, 2005. Then after losing strength crossing Florida, Katrina entered the Gulf of Mexico. Feeding on the unusually warm waters, it grew to a Category 5 hurricane.

On Monday, August 29th at approximately 6:00 A.M., Hurricane Katrina struck the Louisiana Gulf Coast.

Katrina made its second landfall hitting Buras-Triumph, Louisiana as a Category 3 storm with sustained winds in excess of 145 mph at the center and hurricane force winds radiating 120 miles outward. This was the strongest storm ever recorded in the Gulf of Mexico at that time. Severe damage was caused all along the Gulf Coast from Florida to Texas. Over 300,000 homes were destroyed or determined to be no longer habitable.

The 29 foot storm surge that hit the Louisiana shore was more than anyone was prepared for and more than anything in modern history for the area. Almost 2,000 deaths were attributed to Katrina.

At 11 A.M. on the 29th it was reported that a major levee in New Orleans had failed and water was pouring through the 17th Street Canal. The city was beginning to flood. Shortly after the breach, approximately 80% of New Orleans was under water.

In addition to all the damage caused to homes and businesses by the flooding and high winds as Louisiana's system of levees failed, several oil refineries were knocked off line by the storm. It is my understanding that 19% of the United States oil production was affected. Thirty oil platforms were damaged to various degrees and nine oil refineries were closed. Here on New York's Long Island where I live, word quickly spread concerning gasoline shortages.

The television news coverage of Louisiana showed jaw-dropping reports of flooding and devastation. People were swimming from rooftop to rooftop through waters inhabited by alligators and snakes. After two days of watching the depressing damage reports on the news, I was almost relieved to hear the phone ring. It was my friend Barbara. I had agreed to meet her at a cocktail party on the Freeport waterfront.

"Are you still coming? You haven't changed your mind or anything?"

"Of course, I'm still coming."

"I'll be there by eight o'clock," she informed me.

"I'll be there by eight thirty," I replied. "I've been watching the storm reports. The damage is almost beyond comprehension. It will take me a few minutes to get dressed, but I will be there."

It seemed a little incongruous to me to be thinking about martinis and women minutes after watching the hurricane reports but I was going anyway. I really needed to get my mind off everything I had just seen on the television.

Freeport is a harbor area nestled on the south shore of Long Island behind the barrier island of Long Beach. It is home to many recreational fishing boats, both private and charter, and a smattering of commercial fishing enterprises. There are numerous restaurants and bars attracting considerable nightlife especially during the warmer months.

As I started my car for the easy twenty minute drive, I noticed that I was low on gas. I had more than enough to get to Freeport and back, but I believe in keeping my gas gauge in the upper range rather than the lower. I pulled up to the first gas station convenient to my trip and my jaw dropped. Gas prices were $3.50 a gallon up from $1.75 earlier in the day. I left the station looking elsewhere to fuel my car and the reality started to hit me. Several stations were closed after running out of fuel. Others were also at $3.50. The storm's impact was now reaching everyone in the country.

I finally found a station with a short line, only five cars for each of its four pumps. The price was still $1.75. As I gassed up, the attendant said he was going to $3.50 a gallon when he ran out of his current supply which would be soon.

I got to the party when I said I would, but between the hurricane and the gas prices, my head was swimming.

The cocktail party was basically a networking party. A lot of small business people attended in hopes that if ever a need for their services should arise, you will call them. There were accountants and financial planners aplenty, young attorneys hoping to build a practice, small caterers, insurance salesmen, printers, credit card services, etcetera and one overweight young woman running around in a maid's outfit offering her cleaning services.

The cocktail party wasn't exceptionally exciting and most of the conversations were about the storm damage and its effect on fuel prices across the country. The rest of the conversations were sort of "Hi. I'm Fred and what do you do?" The bar/restaurant was a nice place and the setting on the water was beautiful, so I decided to sit back and enjoy my surroundings. There was an attractive barroom and a beautiful outdoor deck area. I really appreciated the lovely summer evening. It was a shame that there wasn't a woman there that I thought would be a good prospect for me. If so, I might have found the party a little more interesting. Did you ever notice that at a gathering such as this, if there is someone you find attractive the conversations become much more stimulating?

Barbara is really a very dear friend to me. She is a tall, attractive brunette who sells insurance for a living, and she is very good at it. We met at a Christmas party held at the office of a mutual friend in 1988. The party was also my last public appearance with my soon to be ex-wife. We had just separated a month earlier.

Barbara and I have been great friends ever since. She was married for a short time which resulted in a wonderful son who she raised on her own.

During the years of our friendship, we have skied together, danced, dined, and gone to the movies but never dated. I'm not sure why. She often uses me as a security blanket. Rather than go somewhere alone where she doesn't know anybody, she invites me so that she has at least one friend there. I think that is why she asked me to join her at this cocktail party.

The best thing about the relationship is that we can talk openly and honestly to each other about anything. She wasn't impressed with the party either and kept apologizing for inviting me. We both left early.

The morning after the party, I spent some time watching the financial shows on television. Everybody was talking about how with nine major refineries down with various degrees of damage because of Katrina there would be gas shortages for about three months until the refineries returned to full operation. This was why gas prices doubled in one day. I was glad I had filled my tank up the night before. (It is interesting to note that here in my area we never ran short on gas. You could buy all you wanted if you paid the price.)

Chapter 2

At this point, I think I should tell you a little about me. I grew up in a nice middle class neighborhood in Brooklyn, New York, the product of wonderful and loving parents. My parents, my younger sister and I weren't rich, but we were happy. After graduating from Brooklyn Technical High School, which was all boys, six thousand of them, I went to Hunter College. Hunter was all women and I was on a program to transfer into City College School of Architecture. Honestly, I was in Hunter's first coed class. There were four thousand women and a few hundred men in the school at that point. After four years at Tech, it took me several months before I could sit still in class but I was too young to know why.

I didn't like Hunter academically, so after one year I transferred to Arizona State University's School of Architecture. I did not graduate in architecture but I did come away with a degree in construction.

The military draft was very active while I was in school during the late 60's. It was a constant threat especially with my changing schools and changing majors. Young men were allowed four years for four year degree programs and five years for five year degree programs. They were not allowed extra time because of changing majors. Between changing schools and changing majors, I was not going to graduate in four years. Architecture was a five year program that took most people six to complete.

I went to draft parties every other week. I saw numerous friends pulled out of school by the draft. So I joined ROTC (Reserve Officer Training Corps) which was the only way the Army would let me stay in school to graduate. The one hour a week of wearing the uniform on the parade ground and an hour of classroom work was bearable. Looking back, the leadership training that I received served me well throughout my life.

Upon graduation from ASU in 1970, I became a Second Lieutenant in the United Sates Army. It took an act of Congress but I was officially an officer and a gentleman. I had requested the Corps of Engineers; after all I had a degree in Construction so I was surprised to receive my assignment to the Quartermaster Corps (supplies).

Quartermaster is usually good duty and with a shooting war going on in Viet Nam, I was not going to complain very loudly. I was always curious about why I did not get Engineers. As I understood the situation, the school had fifty cadets graduating and the Army gave them fifty slots but only one Engineer slot. Another cadet had also requested Engineers. Since his grade point average was two tenths of a point higher than mine, he received first choice. That sounds fair. "What is his degree in?" I asked. "Philosophy" was the reply.

I had a degree in construction and he had a degree in philosophy. He gets Engineers and I get Quartermaster?! It did not make much sense to me but then this was the Army. I figured that I had better get used to this. I hope it made sense to somebody. I walked away, laughing to myself and scratching my head.

My first year in the Army was spent as an instructor at the Quartermaster School in Fort Lee, Virginia. I taught Storage and Depot Operations. I wrote a course on Storage and Depot Operations. I had never been in a real depot in my life. My second year was spent in the glorious Republic of Viet Nam.

Before leaving for Viet Nam, I took some leave to spend a little time at home with my family and then a few days in Tempe, home of Arizona State University, to see some friends. I spent five days of partying, eating and drinking at my college haunts, and then the fateful day arrived. It was time to head to the airport.

It was a beautiful Monday morning, almost too nice to fly to Viet Nam. Before I left the campus, I stopped up at the ROTC office to say hello. It was about eleven o'clock. I had a one o'clock flight from Sky Harbor Airport to San Francisco and a four o'clock flight to Viet Nam. One of the secretaries handed me a piece of paper and asked, "Did you know him?" It was the obituary of a close friend who had just been killed in the Mekong Delta. He was one of my first friends in the dorms when I started at ASU and sat next to me for four years in ROTC. It shook me. The timing was just great. I still think of him today, more than forty years later.

After reaching Viet Nam, I was sent up to Da Nang. Da Nang is located in the northern sector of South Viet Nam along the coast of the South China Sea. Except for the barbed wire, China Beach in Da Nang was one of the most beautiful beaches I had ever been on in my young life. The water was so clear that a person could read a book through six feet of it.

Recently, on the travel channel, I saw a beautiful Hilton Hotel there now. My accommodations were not quite as luxurious. Let me see now. A Quonset hut surrounded by sand bags and barbed wire versus a room at the Hilton. It's a tough decision, but I think I would have preferred the Hilton.

My first day at the beach was also my last as I was assigned to a battalion which processed equipment out of Viet Nam. The office that gave out assignments was about fifty feet from the front door of one of the largest depots in the world. Why wasn't I assigned to the depot? When I asked about an assignment to the depot, the young specialist said "Wow! An Army trained, depot instructor officer. I would love to assign you to the depot but the Colonel who has to approve you is down south for a few days."

"I don't mind waiting. After all, I do have a year to kill."

"Well, you have already been here for a day, and I have to assign you somewhere."

This is the Army, after all, and it turned out that one of the other lieutenants working with me was an Engineer officer. We also had two trained cooks working in the motor pool and two mechanics in the mess hall. The Army probably calls it "cross training." Most other people would call it inefficiency.

For part of the time that I was in Viet Nam, I lived on a Navy compound. The food was great. They actually had trained cooks in the mess hall. Unfortunately, I did not stay there long, and my company moved back to an Army compound. There was a definite difference in the food.

The Navy was much more career oriented than the Army was. A minimum hitch in the Navy was four years and it had a significantly higher retention rate than the Army. The Army was full of draftees who were in for two years, then out. If the Navy needed two cooks, it sent for the next two cooks. If it needed two mechanics, it sent for next two mechanics. The Army said "The next two guys, you are now cooks. The next two guys, you are mechanics."

The war or should I say "conflict" was starting to wind down. The Nixon administration was mired in tense negotiations with the North Vietnamese, the "Paris Peace Talks". We had to get all the equipment out of the country, or when the truce was declared, any remaining equipment would become property of the North Vietnamese.

I ran an operations yard, processing battle-damaged equipment, tanks, trucks, jeeps, howitzers, out of Viet Nam to be repaired and stored elsewhere. The equipment had to be washed to remove any soil or contaminants before it could be shipped out. At one point, I had two hundred men, both GI's and Vietnamese nationals, working under me. The working equipment was processed at another yard just down the road from me.

Basically, I ran a car wash in a junk yard. Another thing the Army taught me which served me well in life is to be flexible.

My time in Viet Nam wasn't glorious by any stretch but I was fairly safe from enemy action, a situation for which

I have always been very grateful. My biggest problems were snakes and dope addicts. My yard was at the base of Monkey Mountain on the Bay of Da Nang, not far from the deep water pier. The Bay of Da Nang opened to the South China Sea.

There were a lot of monkeys on Monkey Mountain, as you might expect, and they would sit in the trees watching us wash junk. During one particular storm, I remember noticing all the monkeys watching us stand out in the rain washing the damaged equipment. They were probably saying to each other "I thought humans were supposed to be smarter than us."

A few weeks after I started at the yard, we had a typhoon, one hundred twenty mile per hour winds and torrential rains for two days. It washed many snakes down the side of the mountain and quite a few took up residence in my yard. During two hours of the first morning after the storm, my sergeant and I killed six snakes, two cobras, two temple vipers (aka two-step Charlies) and two others that we could not identify.

A cobra generally could not kill a man. It had venom that could make a man sick but he could recover. It could kill a small animal or child. Temple vipers, on the other hand, had venom that would paralyze the nervous system within seconds and all bodily functions would cease. The nickname of "Two- Step Charlie" was very appropriate because after two steps you were dead. From then on as I walked around the yard, my eyes were always looking left and right for snakes. Occasionally, I would find one.

My other major problem was dope addicts. At one point I had as many as twenty five percent of my men on smack (heroin.) They would roll the tobacco out of a cigarette, mix in the smack, repack the cigarette and smoke it.

Every month or so, the Army would order a surprise piss test (urine analysis) and the next day a good chunk of my work force was in a detox center.

The only direct fire incident that I experienced was at the hands of one of my sergeants. Three of my E-7's (Sergeants First Class) set up temporary living quarters out of several truck bodies at one end of my yard.

One day while conducting normal operations, I heard some gunfire coming from that direction. Since I had never heard gunfire in my yard before, the sounds got my immediate attention. Moments later two of my men came running up to me saying bullets had just missed their heads. I told everyone to stand back while I went to investigate.

It seemed that one of my sergeants just received notice that he was being riffed. (RIF stands for reduction in force.) He was being laid off by the Army after more than eighteen years of service. You needed twenty for a pension.

As the war was winding down, the Army realized that it did not need as many men anymore and made significant cuts in manpower. The sergeant was understandably upset and possibly inebriated. He picked up a Thompson submachine gun and fired a clip at the walls.

A Thompson fires a .45 caliber bullet at high velocity, a very powerful bullet. The bullets went through the walls of the truck body as if the walls were made of paper. How he had gotten a Thompson was something I never found out. To my knowledge, they were never authorized in Viet Nam.

Fortunately, I was able to convince him to surrender the weapon rather than shoot me. If that negotiation had not ended successfully, who would have written this book? He was removed by the military police a short while later and the yard went back to business as usual.

My respect for the soldiers in the field, who faced snakes, dope addicts, booby traps and trained enemy soldiers trying to kill them on a daily basis, can never be understated.

As for the equipment we processed out, the largest item we handled was the M60 tank. It was the hot new tank in the Army's arsenal at that time. It could go through the jungle at high speed. It weighed fifty tons, one hundred thousand pounds. There was always great pressure on us to get these processed out quickly. No one wanted these tanks left behind. The scrap metal value alone was worth one hundred thousand dollars. That was in 1971 dollars. Money is always such a great motivator.

It seems that several years later, after computers were invented, the M60 was not considered suitable for retrofitting. The new tanks had very sophisticated computer systems. In the 1990's many M60s were dumped in the ocean as part of an artificial reef building program. Apparently, it was cheaper to get rid of them than maintain and keep them in storage.

The cost of putting them in the ocean was three hundred dollars each, dropped in place. What happened to the one hundred thousand dollar scrap metal value? I really cannot complain because I am a big believer in artificial reefs and have enjoyed many days of fishing on them. I wonder if I ever fished on a tank that I washed. I hope the fish appreciate a clean environment.

Upon returning home in 1972, I finally went to work for a construction company. I had intended to go back to

Arizona to build homes, but I didn't have a car or wardrobe at the time. I interviewed for a job here in New York with the intent of going out to Arizona after six months or so. Maybe I would be worth a few dollars more per week if I could say that I was working for a construction company when I finally interviewed out west. A family friend referred me to Starrett Housing Corp.

The job in New York developed into something that did not exist anywhere else in the world. After a short stint in the office, I was sent out to the field for some "seasoning." I started as an assistant superintendent trainee over three buildings at Starrett City in New York. This was a big project consisting of six thousand apartment units in forty-six high-rise buildings, eight five story garages, a power plant and a shopping center.

I loved the field work and it showed. I quickly rose to assistant superintendent over five buildings and then to superintendent over seventeen buildings and finally to Deputy Project Superintendent over the whole job. This job went up faster than anyone expected. In fact, nothing in the world this big had gone up as fast before. During the superstructure phase of the project we averaged fifteen hundred cubic yards of concrete poured in place every day for twelve months. That's a lot of concrete.

I greatly enjoyed the pace and the coordination that was required. It was a wonderful education and a great start to my career. I have always been proud of my participation in the project.

All good things come to an end, and this job did for me in 1976. At some point all construction projects get completed. In 1977 I found myself in commercial real estate in Manhattan. I started leasing office space. At the time I really was not aware of office leasing as a business, but it is a very big business. Working in the city also gave me an opportunity to go back to school at night and between the extra courses I took at ASU and the additional courses I took here, I earned the equivalent of a Masters in Real Estate and enough credits for a third degree.

After five years of working for somebody who taught me everything I didn't want to be in life, I changed companies and wound up co-managing a branch office for a major real estate company. We grew the office from fifteen people to fifty people. It didn't take long for me to find out that bigger offices meant more administration and bigger politics and I don't play the game well. I was doing more and more paperwork and less real estate. Office politics was never my strong suit.

After six years, I left in 1989 and went out on my own working from home. I was focusing on the sale and financing of shopping centers and other investment grade properties across the country. I worked on one deal in particular where the property was in Florida, the developer was in California, the finances came from Seattle and I was in New York. No one cared where my office was. The nice thing about this type of sales is that if you bring someone a property that he likes, he wouldn't care if you lived on a park bench.

In 1996 I put together a large project in Florida for a developer, Bob, with whom I had done business before. The project looked so good that I went into the deal as a partner. We were developing one thousand apartment units in the City of Brandon, just outside of Tampa to the southeast.

All of the zoned properties were expensive, and the sellers wanted to close a sale within thirty days. This was just too quick for us. Right across the street was a large parcel of land, about one hundred ten acres, that was unzoned. It literally had cattle grazing on it. I suggested that we check it out and see what it would take to get the zoning.

The engineers told us that it would take about one year and one hundred thousand dollars to get the zoning approved. The county had just built a new sewage plant to accommodate the anticipated growth and wanted to get us approved quickly so we could start paying fees and taxes to help pay for it. This timing would work perfectly for us. This gave us the time to line up the financing and architectural work so that right after closing we could hit the ground running and start construction.

What is the old saying "Man plans and God laughs?" It took three and a half years and more than three hundred thousand dollars to get the zoning, but we really did not mind. The frustrations kept hitting us in the face because we really wanted to get started but the area was getting more valuable as we waited. Several big banks and insurance companies were opening large office complexes in the area which brought many jobs and the demand for more housing.

We had six months after the zoning approval to close on the land purchase. It was two months before we were scheduled to close on the purchase of the property when I received a phone call from one of our associates in California. Bob had died of an abdominal aneurism. He was four months younger than I was at the time. His death really jolted me. Younger friends weren't supposed to be dying.

As far as the project was concerned, I felt that I was more than capable of bringing it to completion. The problem was that no bank was going to give me seventy-five million dollars to build this project without my having a track record as a developer, so the project died too. Between deposits and fees, we left more than three million dollars cash on the table.

Things were great for a while, but between 2001 and 2002 I hit burnout. I was goosed by people I trusted on two major deals. On one deal I could have sued for my commission which would have been in seven figures but I was so burnt that I just turned around and walked away. If I had it to do all over again, there is no doubt in my mind that I would definitely sue.

At this point I was somewhat broke and slightly depressed, but I never learned to quit, so I put one foot in front of the other and did whatever I had to do to survive.

I drove an older car. It was a 1992 Crown Victoria with one hundred forty thousand miles on the engine. It was sluggish and the engine had a tappet noise that sounded like a typewriter and I was not a mechanic. Every two weeks it was in the shop for something. Finally, I decided that it was time to buy another car but, I was so busy that I did not go out and buy one the next day.

A few days later, I found myself at a sport fishing trade show. At one of the booths, I saw a lubricant demonstrated. It was an oil additive. I was intrigued by the demonstration and bought some for my car. As I said I am not a mechanic but I knew what I saw was good. What did I have to lose? After I added the product to the engine, the car was peppy.

It was fun coming to a stop sign and stepping on the gas again. The engine was quiet and smooth.

I was so impressed by the product that I called the company. Really now, how many times in a lifetime are you so impressed by a product that you call the company? I don't think that I had ever done that before. (By the way, I kept that car for another five years and put an additional eighty-five thousand miles on it. The engine and transmission were fine. I never did an engine repair during that time but everything else on the car was going.)

I wound up speaking to the local regional distributor who was a wonderful guy but not a salesman, so we sat down one day and worked out a deal and my new career was underway.

The product line is not generally a fast sell, except for me, I guess. Accounts didn't come rolling in from day one so I wound up driving a limo for an airport transportation company at night and on weekends. I was working seventy to eighty hours a week driving and another thirty hours selling lubricants. I didn't have any trouble falling asleep. Eventually, I was able to cut back on the driving as sales picked up.

As for my recreational life, I have no shortage of interests. I am an avid saltwater fisherman. This is a love I developed as a kid from going fishing with my father. My father managed a nursing home which was family-owned. He was on call seven days a week, but every now and then he would take a day off during the week and go fishing. I would cut a day of first or second grade and go with him. I would almost always get seasick, but I didn't mind. I was fishing with my father.

When I returned home from the Army, I continued my fishing, eventually finding a nice fishing club in which I have been very active for almost thirty years.

Somewhere along the line I took up the cause against the potting of blackfish. The official name for the fish is tautog, one of my favorite fish to fish for. Blackfish are among the smartest fish in the sea. They will take your bait and spit the hook very quickly. To hook the fish, it takes a lot of practice to get the timing right. Catching them with any consistency is an accomplishment.

In the late 1980's a market developed for live blackfish. The market price for live blackfish was more than most commercial fishermen could resist. The price jumped from fifty cents a pound to between three and four dollars a pound for live fish. A fisherman, by using fish pots, could catch and keep the blackfish alive. The nice thing about fish pots from the commercial fisherman's perspective is that you don't have to be there for them to work. The pot just sits on the bottom catching fish. The fisherman comes along once a week and empties the pot.

One commercial fisherman standing on a street corner in Sheepshead Bay in Brooklyn told me he had twelve hundred pots working for him out at Montauk Point. Montauk Point is one hundred twenty miles away due east. The wide use of fish pots has decimated the biomass.

My fight brought me to the Marine Resources Advisory Council, an advisory arm to the New York State Division of Environmental Conservation. After speaking to the Council on my views regarding fish pots, I was invited to join the council. It seems that there was a vacancy at one of the recreational slots. The MRAC consists of seven people from various aspects of commercial fishing and seven people from various aspects of recreational fishing with a chairman in the middle. The goal of the Council is to be a sounding board for the DEC and to help sustain the fisheries for all purposes. I sat for five years on the Council and I currently sit on a Federal advisory panel.

Apparently, when I find a cause that I believe in, I mount my trusty steed, grab my lance and attack the windmills.

I am an active golfer, or at least was. Three years ago, I was just getting my game to break ninety with some regularity when my chief golf partner and coach passed away. Without his calling me and nagging me to go, I just haven't played as often. Golf always cost me the whole day and with tennis, another hobby, I found that I could play in the morning and be back in my office by nine thirty or ten.

A friend referred me to a very nice group of tennis players. I currently play three mornings a week which is about as much as my body can handle. I am not a great player but I have a lot of fun at an intermediate level. The exercise is big plus. My passion for photography cannot be overlooked. I am also a reasonably accomplished amateur photographer.

My current business is selling automotive and mechanical lubricants. The products are among the best in the world at what they do. It gives a salesman great confidence when he walks into someone's office knowing he has the best products in the world.

Most salesmen can adapt themselves to selling any item whether it is suits or ice cream. I could never do that. I have to believe in the product. My word and my credibility are very important to me. I could never rep a second-rate product and go around telling everyone how wonderful it was. I consider myself a serviceman, not a salesman. Someone has a need and I have a product to help him. The product can be an office building, shopping center or a lubricant.

The oil additive will drop the load factor on the engine (make it work easier at the same rpms), protect against dry starts where about eighty percent of engine wear occurs, extend the life of the engine and save approximately ten percent in fuel. I also offer grease and a diesel fuel additive.

Chapter 3

On the morning after the cocktail party, I had an eleven o'clock appointment with the head mechanic of a small trucking firm (25 trucks +/-) located at the Inwood fuel terminal just south of John F. Kennedy Airport, about a fifteen minute drive from my home. It was a bright sunny day, and I felt good about the prospects of landing a new customer. I was naively optimistic in the beginning of my new career.

As I cleared the security gate of the terminal, my customer was located to my left, on the east side of the yard. The company had a dispatch office and a small truck maintenance shop. All of their trucks said Sunoco on them but trucks with various brand and non-brand names were filling up from the same pipelines, so much for the differences between one gasoline brand and another. Together with other brand offices, they formed a perimeter around the fueling station.

At any time of day or night, you can see fuel trucks running up and down Peninsula Boulevard to fill up and deliver their gasoline to points throughout much of Long Island. I had left some of my products with Jack, the head mechanic, on my last visit, and was hoping to hear some positive feedback and land a new customer. I entered the office and a slightly overweight gentleman, about fifty or so, was on the telephone, laughing about how many of his gas stations had run dry the night before and that they were getting $3.50 a gallon. He did not seem concerned about the impending shortages due to Katrina.

It is important to understand that the stations ran dry, not because there was a shortage of gas but because so many people anticipated a shortage and ran to top off their tanks. The stations were all back on line the next morning.

When the gentleman noticed me and realized that some of his conversation was being overheard, his laughing voice became much more business-like.

"What can I do for you?" he asked gruffly.

"I have an appointment with Jack." I replied with a pleasant smile on my face. He, not so pleasantly, directed me to Jack in the shop. Jack was impressed with my products but I had to talk to his boss, the owner, who didn't like to spend money even if I could save him money. (Where did I hear this one before?)

All the way back to my office, I kept thinking that something didn't ring true. If these people who supplied my region with fuel did not seem concerned about the gas shortages, why was everybody else concerned? These people knew more about their inventories and supply chain than anyone else did. Shouldn't they be somewhat anxious about the situation? The mood in the office was outright jovial.

I like to think of myself as a bright person. I am not educated in all areas, but I catch on after a while. This just did not make any sense to me. From the car, I called Barbara to thank her for inviting me to last night's party and related my confusion from this morning's visit to the terminal.

"It doesn't make any sense. These people were outright giddy about the run on gasoline."

"You mean they weren't concerned?"

"If they were, they had a funny way of showing it."

"I'm sorry about last night. I thought the party would be more interesting."

"Don't worry about it. I'm on to bigger and better things." I am not sure what things exactly.

I returned to my home where I maintain my office. I converted an extra bedroom to office space. There are definite advantages to a ten foot commute to work in the morning. The commute is very short, and I do not have to get dressed to go to work except if I have appointments out of the office. You would be amazed at the telephone discussions that I have had while in various states of undress.

While my morning radio might be reporting all the traffic tie-ups on the Long Island Expressway, at the Lincoln and Battery Tunnels, at all the bridges and highways, I could not care less. However, I do miss having the usual water cooler conversations about the game last night or the front page of the newspaper. Sometimes the highlight of my day is going to the post office.

When I left my office in the city, my biggest concern about working from home was would I stay up late to watch the late movie and then sleep late the next morning. Before I'd know it, it's three in the afternoon and I would still be walking around in my underwear. It is impossible to be productive that way, so I get up early every morning and go out for breakfast. It gets me dressed and sets my day in motion.

I sit at the counter of my local coffee shop and solve all the problems of the world with the other regulars and then head to the office at nine. It works for me. The walk to the coffee shop helps compensate for the exercise I lose by working from home. My home is located just outside of the center of town. It's a short walk to the post office, bank, diner and pizzeria. I love it.

The financial shows on television were all talking about the ramifications of Katrina and showing the incredible amount of damage left in its wake. How was this going to affect the markets and which stocks would benefit and which stocks would not? Everybody was an expert and everybody had an opinion. Please note that many of these expert opinions disagreed with many of the other expert opinions. The interesting aspect of these "experts" is that if one said buy and the other said sell the odds are that one of them would be right.

The Supreme Court has long held that there is no such thing as an illegal opinion. In other words, if I say "You are a crook" I can be sued and held liable unless I can prove that you are a crook. But if I say "In my opinion you are a crook" there is nothing that you can do about it. You are allowed to have any opinion you want. Could this be why so many "experts" are so eager to offer their opinions?

The expected ninety day downtime for the damaged refineries was going to cause fuel shortages. Gas prices doubled overnight and were expected to stay at the $3.50 level during the next three months until the refineries came back on line. Gasoline prices jumped, but there was no significant move in oil prices. There was plenty of fuel.

After the initial run on gas on the first night after the storm, I never saw a gas line or a gas station closed because of no fuel. People griped at the price of gas but they bit the bullet and paid it. Putting out fifty, sixty or seventy dollars to fill the tank cuts down on one's cash on hand. It limits spending money especially if there is more than one car in the household, but for three months we could live with it.

It was almost ninety days exactly when the refineries came back on line, and the price at the pump started back down. It is interesting to note that almost all of the refineries came back on line at the same time. Is that just coincidence? Maybe, maybe not.

I would have guessed that some of the repairs may have been completed in a week, some in a month, some in two months, some in three months and that fuel prices would have started down after a month or so until things got back to normal. Heck, what do I know?

Here on Long Island prices got as low as $2.50 to $2.25. Not quite back to the $1.75 level but a lot better than $3.50. Then the world shook. Gasoline prices went straight up to $4 and $5 a gallon. What the heck was going on? There were no strikes at the refineries. No OPEC (Organization of Petroleum Exporting Countries) country was being overthrown by rebels. There were no oil fields afire. What was going on?

Back on the financial news shows, all the interviewees were saying that it was India and China. The growing industrialization of India and China was demanding more oil and causing the price to rise.

This didn't make any sense to me at all. Granted, India and China were growing. Their economies were growing. No argument. But they did not surge unexpectedly overnight. This was bull! True, I am no expert on global economics but I had a tough time swallowing this.

Every significant investment firm had a team of people watching the economies of India and China on a daily basis. They usually have teams watching every industrialized nation as well as the emerging nations. Everybody could not have missed something this big. There is no way that I could accept the claim that this spike in fuel prices was because of India and China.

Chapter 4

The limo job wasn't my primary goal as far as careers are concerned, but the money helped until the lubricant business could support me. At least this company dealt with a better class clientele, primarily vacationers and business travelers. I was not interested in taking drunks home when the bars closed or taking teenagers on drug buys. Gratefully, this company did not have any of that business. We had a lot of regulars, many of whom I became casual friends with. Some people were fairly interesting, and we had many thought provoking conversations. I would try to pick brains when I could find them. I love to learn about fields of business and products that I would not otherwise come across. Often, I would give as well as I got.

One passenger was regional head of distribution for a major pharmaceutical company. He had just come from a seminar introducing a new antiangiogenesis cancer drug.

Angiogenesis refers to blood flow and antiangiogenesis is the stopping of blood flow. The pill would stop the blood flow to certain cancerous tumors and the tumors would die leaving the patient healthy and cancer free. Instead of long term care in a hospital the patient can come in to the hospital once a month and take a pill. There were no side effects like those related to radiation and chemotherapy. The cost per pill was several thousand dollars but this was much, much cheaper than a month's stay at a hospital for chemo treatments and more effective. It was cheaper than one day's stay.

He was very excited about it and I found it very interesting especially since I had a distant cousin who was very involved in the research for many years. You just don't hear terms like antiangiogenesis thrown around the coffee shop or pizzeria very often.

Sometimes people who got in my car would open up to me as if I were their shrink. There were quite a few people who would have great conversations with me as if we were long lost brothers. As soon as they were out of the car I was just a lowly driver. The interesting thing is that I could spot most of those people at least twenty IQ points.

One in particular was a college professor. Let's call him Dr. Dan. He was in his sixties, reasonably trim and reeked of arrogance and pomposity. I think he colored his hair with black shoe polish. He made an excellent additional living as a speaker giving seminars around the world. He also considered himself quite the lady's man and would often take a lady friend on a trip. He had degrees in economics, business and political science, in what order I don't remember (and don't care.) I would argue pitting most of his theories against my realities. I actually enjoyed it. He believes that there should not be any social security system. Every person should plan for himself. After all, he did.

I tried to explain to him that not everybody was a doctorate in economics and sometimes a person can get caught in someone else's fraud through no fault of his own. Did you ever hear of Enron or World Com? Not everybody made several hundred thousand dollars a year. What should we do with our elderly? How about we just leave them on a street corner with a loaf of bread and a bottle of water? Maybe the sanitation department can sweep up the bodies after a few days. Dr. Dan is such an ass.

I picked him up from the airport one time when he was returning from Bulgaria. I asked him how they were doing with their conversion to capitalism. He replied that he thought they were going in the right direction but it would take a generation to remove the old ways of thinking from interfering with the new progressive plans.

I told him that Moses spent forty years in the desert for the same reason. Old embittered minds would die off or be too old to be effectual, thereby allowing younger minds, not poisoned by the bitterness of slavery in Egypt, to flourish in a new setting. Dan thought that was brilliant and asked if he could use it in his lectures. Of course, I allowed him. It's a shame I couldn't get royalties. I wonder what his reaction would have been if I said no?

After Dr. Dan, I had another call picking up a couple from American Airlines at JFK going back to Rockville Centre. Rockville Centre is a very nice town with a very nice town center. There were many restaurants and bars and the nightlife was good especially on the weekends. Rockville Centre is a little more monied than my town of Lynbrook.

Tommy was my favorite dispatcher and I was his favorite driver. He always tried to keep me busy. I don't know if it was because I was so good or most of the other drivers weren't. Tommy was retired after thirty years as a mechanic for the New York City sanitation department. While he was still working for sanitation, he would pull a second shift driving a van for the airport service. He always had a pillow with him in the van. If he had time between calls he would grab some sleep. Most of us learned to sleep in the vehicles when we had the time.

When he retired from sanitation, he took the dispatcher position. He smokes too much and doesn't eat right and recently had a heart attack, but we have been friendly ever since I started working there. He gave up smoking and caffeine after the heart attack. That lasted several weeks then he went back to all his bad habits. Some people never learn.

By the time I got back to the airport, the other couple was waiting for me with their bags. The gentleman appeared to be in his late forties and his wife slightly younger. Both were tall, attractive and well dressed. They maintained very proper airs about them. I wondered if they had sex with their clothes on. He told me that he was a stock broker for Merrill Lynch. Naturally, I brought up the gasoline situation.

He "knew" that the run up in prices was because of India and China. I told him that I believed that was what he had been told but that it did not make any sense. India and China were growing but their economies did not go poof and triple in size overnight. "It's definitely India and China. We follow this very closely at the office."

I wanted to tell him that I believed his office followed India and China very closely and that is why I do not think India and China had anything to do with fuel prices jumping so suddenly. After a few minutes, I could not resist, and told him.

"If your firm watched India and China so closely, how come they missed this explosive growth that has driven fuel prices so high? India and China had nothing to do with this." I smiled as I politely disagreed with him. I tried not to sound too harsh, but I hate when people show off their ignorance. Besides, he hadn't tipped me yet.

Many of the investment firms had teams of analysts following India and China on a full time basis. Some analysts even lived in the respective countries. There is just no way that the economies of India and China jumped up so dramatically overnight and nobody saw it coming.

We arrived at their house and I helped them to the door with their bags. He offered me his business card in case I wanted to invest. I took it graciously and said thank you. I haven't called him yet. I wonder if he is waiting by the phone for my call.

Chapter 5

Through most of 2006, oil prices climbed, approaching $80 by late summer before falling back to the $50 range by year's end. Then from the beginning of 2007, prices went straight up, reaching a high of $147 per barrel in July of 2008. The year 2007 was particularly hard for most people as the shock of high oil prices started to have major effects on their lives. This time it was not going to be for three months. This time it was going to be for a much longer period.

What was driving these prices up? Previously, oil prices rose because of workers striking at the oil fields, rebel attacks, oil field fires, embargos, wars or some other outside event, but nothing like that was happening. Things just didn't make any sense to me. There was no shortage. All the gasoline you wanted was available. Nobody on the news shows had any answers. A lot of people were saying India and China but I still could not give that argument any credibility. Who was doing this?

Many people in the general public blamed the Arabs for the spike in oil prices. I remember seeing the President of OPEC on the news one night in the fall of 2007. Oil was about $75 per barrel at that point. He was crying that "We are not doing this. It is not us. Forty to fifty dollars a barrel offered more than enough profit for everyone. We are not doing this. It must be the traders or someone else. We are not doing this."

I am sure that he had no concern for my monthly budget, but I found myself believing him. Who was doing this?

My home is a nothing special high ranch, a very typical house here on suburban Long Island. I used to be warm for $150 a month worth of heating oil; now I was cold for $650 a month. I had the thermostat turned down so low trying to save oil that I thought it was going to snow in the living room. I would watch television wearing two hooded sweatshirts and a blanket. My electric bill jumped from $100 per month to $300 or more. Long Island Power Authority passed the cost of their fuel directly through to customers. It is also the most expensive electric service in the country.

Everything in the stores was more expensive because the merchandise was trucked in. Most truckers added fuel surcharges to their fees. In a typical two car household, monthly gas expenses went up about $150 per car. Forget what ethanol did to food prices. All the corn was going to ethanol processors and some wheat fields switched to the now more lucrative corn. This drove the cost of feed grain for livestock through the roof as well as wheat flour for pizza, pasta, bagels, and bread. Beef, chicken, pork and pasta prices rose significantly.

The higher grain prices had a significant effect around the world as American surplus grain feeds many people.

If you add it all up, the average household budget went up by about $1500 per month of after-tax dollars. That equals $2500 before taxes which is the same as taking a $30,000 cut in annual pay. This is also enough to finance a three hundred to three hundred fifty thousand dollar mortgage. Most people, who bought homes recently, did not have an extra three hundred thousand dollars of mortgage power in their budget. I spoke with many people in the area, and everybody agreed with my analysis and several noted their expenses were higher.

What a coincidence, home sales came to a standstill about the same time. Very few people seemed to notice the correlation between oil prices and home sales. None of the financial talk shows, that I am aware of, ever mentioned the connection.

Understand that we were in a violently upward housing market for the last several years. Home prices were spiraling out of sight as banks made more and more mortgage money available. The reasons for this I will touch upon shortly. People were stretching to their limits and beyond to buy a home before they would be passed by. They might never again be able to afford a house.

Home buyers were being steered into adjustable rate mortgages with low starting rates. The lower starting rates allowed people to qualify for mortgages that they would not have been able to qualify for otherwise. At three percent a person can qualify for a larger mortgage than he can at seven percent. When the bank sells the adjustable rate mortgage it makes three times the profit over the sale of a fixed rate mortgage. The buyers had no idea what they were doing and many a mortgage broker took advantage. I am always cautious when prices go up too quickly. I have seen them come down just as quickly.

I spoke to at least fifty people who were passengers in my car who told me they had adjustable rate mortgages. When I asked what their interest rate adjustment was tied to, only one of them had any idea what I was talking about. He was a Chief Financial Officer of his company and took an adjustable rate mortgage which was fixed for five years and then adjusted. He didn't know what index it was tied to or how it would adjust and he didn't care. He took the adjustable rate mortgage because his son was graduating from law school the next year and he expected to sell his house and downsize within three years. He took advantage of the lower starting rate and did not expect to be around when it adjusted.

None of these people had any idea what the interest rate and mortgage payment would be after it adjusted. Interestingly, I had not heard of anyone's mortgage payment adjusting down.

Most adjustable rate mortgages have rates that move up or down based upon one of several different indexes. For example, take treasury rates. If a mortgage is tied to a particular treasury bond rate and that rate was up or down at a specific point in time, the interest rate would adjust accordingly. Other common indexes are the prime rate, London Interbank Overnight Rate (LIBOR), federal district cost of funds. The mortgage could have fixed increases after a certain date was reached. Usually there is a spread over the index. For example, if the spread was two percent over the index and the index was at six percent, then the new rate would be eight percent.

Ninety-nine percent of the people had no idea how their interest rate would adjust or whether they would be able to afford the mortgage when it did adjust. The mortgage brokers told them, "If the mortgage adjusts too high, simply refinance." That sounds great but what was the rate going to be at some point in the future when they went to refinance? Would their incomes allow them to qualify for the new mortgage at that time? Nobody knows.

They were lambs lining up for the slaughter. Now their monthly budgets were getting rocked for $1500 a month more, not counting the mortgage adjustment. Some people did not have it. Heck, many did not have it. The increase in oil prices was about to have a big effect on these people, not to mention the rest of the world.

Ninety percent of us or more live on a budget, so very few of us can absorb a budget increase like this without blinking. For people with a household income of one hundred fifty thousand dollars or less who had just bought a home, taking what equates to a thirty thousand dollar cut in pay could be deadly. It did not matter whether they put a down payment of zero percent or thirty percent. The down payment was insignificant. It was the total monthly expenses that were more important.

I had my buddy, the arrogant Dr. Dan, as a passenger again. I asked him what he thought about the increase in fuel prices. Dan saw no problem. It was hard for me to believe that he could not see a problem with such an increase in fuel prices. How could he have a doctorate degree in economics and not be able to see a problem? How many classes did he cut when he was a student?

"This will help money circulate," he spouted. "It's good. In theory people pay money to the oil companies and the oil companies pay dividends to their shareholders. The shareholders spend the money in stores so the money keeps circulating."

Is he nuts?!

I asked him "How does taking money from three hundred million people and redistributing it to fifty thousand people recirculate money?"

He responded, "Well, I said, in theory, that's how it works."

"Screw theories. In reality there is no reality in your theory. It can't work." I gagged at some of his statements.

"For some unexplained reason, I did not see Exxon at the mall last weekend nor did I see Chevron at the coffee shop this morning. None of that money was coming back to Long Island. You can't take $1500 per household per month out of the economy without major ramifications. If this keeps up," I told him, "you will see the biggest recession in history occur and it won't be only here in the United States. It will be global! It will probably be worse than the 1930's." He just sat there a little less pompous. How much does he get paid to espouse his theories? Good thing he works for academia. How would he ever keep a job in the real world?

"People are stretched to the walls to afford a house in this market. If these fuel prices stay up, you are going to see a lot of foreclosures."

I loved opposing his theories. When I would poke holes in his theories, it was like opening the car window and letting some pomposity out.

In December of 2007, I attended an award ceremony for my alma mater. Each year Arizona State University presents a very prestigious award to the economist who predicts four major indexes for four consecutive years and gets the closest to the actual results. The ceremony is held here in New York. That year the winner was, for the purposes of this book, let's call him Dr. Martin Mason of Viewall Economics. As part of the presentation, the recipient usually presents his views on the upcoming year.

I arrived a few minutes early (I always do) and had the pleasure of speaking with Dr. Mason before the ceremony. I asked him what affect the increase in fuel prices would have on the economy.

"I think it will be negligible, and I do not see any recession looming," he replied. That answer shook me.

"Don't you think that taking fifteen hundred dollars a month per household out of the economy will have a significant effect? I think you are going to see the biggest recession in your life. It will probably be worse than the Great Depression of the 1930's."

He thought for a moment cocking his head slightly to one side and said with a straight face "I'm doing a presentation as part of the award ceremony. Please don't say anything."

I just stood there looking at him. I was stunned. There was nothing I could say.

What was his presentation? First, it is important for you to understand the definition of a recession. A recession is defined as the GDP (gross domestic product - which is the value of all goods and services sold in the country) going down by two percent or more for two quarters in a row. Dr. Mason predicted for 2008, in December of 2007, that consumer spending would go down by four hundred fifty billion dollars and oil revenues would go up by three hundred fifty billion dollars. Therefore the net effect would be no significant dip in the GDP and thus no recession.

Nobody in the audience challenged him during the brief question and answer period. He had a few questions asked of him but nobody challenged his theories. He would not call on me when I raised my hand. I wonder why?

The economy was in freefall, but since it had not reached the technical definition of a recession, no one wanted to use the word. Understand that a "recession" is when the economy is going down. A "depression" is when it is down and stays down. The term "depression" was banned from usage by universal decree and, to my knowledge, was never used during this entire period of "prolonged recession."

I guess that the term "depression" was too depressing and had too many political ramifications.

One month before 2008, Dr. Mason could not see the looming recession. He was standing on the door step of the biggest economic event in his lifetime, and yet he could not see it coming. My mind was doing cartwheels.

How much does this guy get paid and who pays him and why? How high off ground level is his office? He obviously can't see the man on the street. Maybe he and Dr. Dan went to the same school. I bet they cut classes together. I bet they each got A's in Monday morning quarterbacking.

After an economic event happened, they would probably be able to give you several good reasons as to why it happened, but while those reasons were happening, they had no clue that those reasons would cause the economic event.

In January of 2008, it was as if somebody turned the light switch off. Many of my customers, especially those in the construction and concrete business, stopped cold. With homes sales coming to a halt, new home construction slowed to a standstill. When you suddenly lose fifteen hundred dollars a month per household from discretionary spending, the world starts to slow down. The first thing to go is restaurants. It is a lot easier to make a chicken dinner at home for three dollars per person than go out to eat for twenty dollars each.

I was in my friend's restaurant one afternoon in the spring of 2008 when a man came in to service the dishwasher. He said he was receiving three phone calls a week from restaurants asking him to pick up their dishwashers because they were going out of business. This meant that the staffs are being laid off. Laid off people do not spend as much as working people. Wholesalers were starting to cut back and were laying off workers. Many manufacturers were cutting back or closing up. Some were never to reopen.

One driver for a major food wholesaler told me that the company reduced the number of different items that they carried by twenty five percent and cut fifteen percent of their drivers. Discretionary sales all across the spectrum started to dry up. I could use a new dining room table but the old one still works. Spending by many families narrowed to essentials only.

The snowballs were coming down the mountain.

As sales slacked off, more businesses cut back and laid people off or simply went out of business. The more people who were out of work, the more sales dropped. The more sales dropped, the more people got laid off. Every city, state, county and village in America counts on sales tax revenues for a significant portion of its income. As sales dropped off, the revenue stream from sales taxes began to dry up. Income tax revenues also dropped. Unemployed people do not pay a lot in income taxes. You do not pay a lot of income taxes for businesses that lose money. Everybody started cutting back. It was a vicious downward spiral.

Additionally, every municipality saw its expenses go up as fuel prices climbed. Fuel had been running at about one dollar fifty cents per gallon and now was running at four dollars or more. Now multiply this difference by how many gallons of fuel the city, county or state uses.

Incomes going down and expenses going up; it is the magic formula for financial stress. This simple formula worked for virtually every village, city, county, and state in the union as well as for the federal government. Everybody was stressed.

Every now and then one of my customers would tell me that sales had actually picked up but it was always because one of their competitors went out of business. Some of the competitor's business would come their way. Some went elsewhere.

The last man standing will do very well.

Many construction contractors took jobs at a loss just to slow their decline until times got better whenever that might be. Most contractors have offices and equipment to be maintained and key personnel to keep employed. If they did not keep the key people and equipment, if and when they won a contract, it would be hard to perform.

The cost of maintaining the office, property, equipment, and key personnel might be three or four million dollars a year. By taking on a job at a loss, they may slow their losses to one or two million per year and thereby extend how long they could stay in business. There were plenty of contractors who closed up shop permanently. Not everybody was capable of carrying such an overhead for a prolonged period.

I was testing my products at two cities in New Jersey. They saw great results. Equipment ran smoother and consumed less fuel. However, they could not buy my products because of budget cuts. The superintendent of one city told me that he was only allowed to buy products absolutely necessary to make the vehicles run. In other words, he can buy all the brake shoes he needs whenever he needs them but he cannot buy an additive that would save fuel, reduce breakdowns and save money.

Only one municipality stayed with me throughout the recession. The Village of Garden City credits my products with saving it a great deal of money because of the reduced breakdowns and fuel savings. I think Garden City was able to stay with me because it was able to manage its own finances throughout the recession without New York State taking control. The village scrimped and saved wherever it could, but was smart enough not to cut my products.

Some of the other communities that I was dealing with needed state assistance to get by but with the assistance comes state oversight and control.

The oversight very often came in the form of "No, you cannot buy anything."

One county in New Jersey wanted to test my products but was not allowed to buy anything because of budget restrictions. I offered the products for free in order for them to run a test but they were not allowed to accept that. I put together a special "test kit" with about seven hundred dollars worth of products. I offered it to them for the special test kit price of one hundred dollars. No good. For the last four years they have not been able to come up with one hundred dollars to do the testing.

Chapter 6

2007 was a great year for my business. Truckers were panicking over the cost of fuel. Everybody was trying to cut fuel costs. People who slammed the phone down on me two years before were inviting me for lunch, figuratively speaking. I almost tripled my sales from the year before. I wasn't getting rich yet, but I could see making a living in my future. Then zap! 2008 was devastating. Everything came to a grinding halt.

I had been pitching New York City's Department of Sanitation since February 2002. It has six thousand heavy pieces of equipment. That is more equipment than most armies of the world. We independently reached the same estimates as far as savings were concerned. We anticipated that they would spend three to four million dollars a year on my oil additive alone and it would save the Department thirty to forty million dollars. This did not count what my grease, fuel additive, or filter systems would save them.

Their street sweepers had to be washed down every day and regreased because the grease they were using washes off. The machines have thirty-four grease ports on them. I gave the Department several tubes of my grease to test. "Try this stuff. It doesn't wash off. You may get several washings out of it."

They put my grease on the worst bearings on one side of the machine and used their grease on everything else. They got thirty washings out of my grease and then had to add a bead of grease about two inches long to the bearing. If that was ten percent of what was in the bearing, my grease just outperformed their grease by three hundred to one. The test results went into a drawer and, to my knowledge, never resurfaced.

In early 2002, the city was very involved with the cleanup of the World Trade Center and could not focus on the testing of new products. I waited. As the cleanup was completed, eleven hundred members of the Department retired because of all the overtime they logged. Their pensions are greatly affected by the final year's salary. The overtime pay put most of these people at salary levels they would never see again. Anybody eligible for retirement, including the head of the section that I was dealing with, did and I could not blame them.

I had to wait for the new administration and his entourage to become entrenched. We are not talking of waiting for hours. We are talking years.

Over the years, the city tried my products whenever a problem would arise such as when a certain bearing or gear would fail prematurely on a number of vehicles. My products always solved the problem, but I could not get the Department to move forward. Finally, in 2008, I got the big boss to agree to formally test my products. We set up a meeting for the following week.

It was a cold and wet January morning, but I felt as if it were a warm, sunny day. The meeting was called for seven in the morning. I didn't pick the time, they did but I didn't care. I would have been there at any time day or night they picked. Their group starts at five-thirty, so it could have been worse. I allowed a lot of extra time for traffic or anything else that might hold me up. I did not want to be late for this meeting.

There is a gas station with a coffee shop around the corner from their building, and I stopped there for some breakfast. I was very early as usual and I thought that it was a good way to kill some time and settle my stomach.

The Department of Sanitation building is a very large maintenance facility in Woodside, Queens just off the Long Island Expressway. The entrance to the part of the building where I was going was at the top of a very large ramp. The ramp was built for large garbage trucks to use and went straight from the street level to the fourth floor with a security guard at the top. At 6:45 AM I headed up the ramp. I tried to drive past the security guard quietly so as not to wake him. I am very courteous like that.

The meeting was held in their conference room. The décor was on the functional side and not designed to impress visitors with its opulence. Nobody could accuse them of wasting money on decorators.

The boss was sitting at one end of the conference table and I was at the other end. There were eight members of his posse between us. Finally the words I was waiting for were spoken. "Fred, you watch the oil additive. Charlie, you watch the grease. Sam, you watch the fuel additive and Bert, you keep an eye on the filter systems." Meeting adjourned. It took all of five minutes, not counting the six years it took to get the meeting. I was elated. It took great effort on my part to keep a businesslike persona on the outside, but inside I was flying. It was hard to keep my heart inside my chest.

The ride home was in heavy rush hour traffic, but I really did not notice.

I called the next morning to set up the tests and my world was shattered. The city had just passed an edict banning the testing of any new products. The next morning! It seems the reduced income tax and sales tax revenues combined with the city's increased expense for fuel caused the city to drastically tighten its belt to meet its budget. Testing of new products was out. No exceptions.

One of the posse members told me "Even if you paid for the testing, we could not justify the time it would take to read the results."

My house is only two stories so jumping out of a window would only cause a sprained ankle at most and a few scratches from landing in the bushes. I might have jumped off a bridge, but I did not want to waste the gas to get to one high enough to do the trick. So I put one foot in front of the other and continued to march.

Fortunately, I keep a low overhead for my business. Everything went into survival mode. My office is in my house and I keep a small storage facility elsewhere. If I had to maintain an office out of the house and pay conventional rents, the odds are that I would have been out of business. I have been able to expand my territory as other distributors closed up shop. You could see "For Rent" signs going up on many major shopping streets. Vacancy rates started to go up for office space as well. Job losses were running at seven hundred thousand per month nationally.

I wanted to call Dr. Mason and see if he noticed any recession, although technically, by definition, we were not in a recession yet. Could he tell if the rising cost of fuel was having an effect on the world economy? I was curious to know what his prediction for 2009 was. His crystal ball was probably made in China.

As oil prices soared to a high of one hundred forty seven dollars a barrel in July of 2008, mortgages started to fail at a rate of ten to twelve percent. It is important for you to understand something of the mortgage banking business, so please allow me to give you a simplified crash course.

The traditional home mortgage failure rate is one tenth of one percent. That's one failure for every one thousand mortgages. If you take out mortgage insurance, which is often required, it generally costs a quarter of one percent of the amount of the mortgage. This covers the one tenth of one percent failure rate plus the fees and profits to everyone along the line. Your bank then sells off your mortgage. An adjustable rate mortgage brings in three times as much profit to the bank as a fixed rate mortgage does.

An investor would rather buy something where the income increases over time rather than stays flat. This is why the banks were pushing adjustable mortgages over fixed. Many were pushing adjustable mortgages to the point of lying about the rates on fixed rate mortgages.

Promise them anything but make sure they take an adjustable mortgage.

Someone collects these mortgages from the banks, puts them into large bundles and resells them to investment banks, hedge funds and other investment groups. With the low failure rate and the mortgage insurance, the bundles were considered so safe that the purchasers received forty to one leverage. This means that by putting one billion dollars down, they could buy forty billion dollars in mortgages. The bundles were paying approximately six and a half to seven percent from the outset plus upside as the adjustable rates kicked in.

The remaining thirty nine billion was financed with margin financing at a cost of about two and one half percent. It's like when you buy a stock on margin, only much more leveraged. The investment bank has an income of six and a half percent and an expense of two and a half percent. This provides a four point spread for the investment bank. That means that the purchase of the bundle of mortgages for forty billion dollars putting one billion down would produce a profit of approximately four percent or one billion six hundred million dollars every year plus upside and it was fully insured. What a game!

Can you imagine investing one billion dollars once and making back one billion six hundred million and more each year for many years to come? This is what was driving the mortgage market.

This is why the investment banks kept putting pressure on the home mortgage lenders to push out more and more mortgages so investment banks could leverage up and make huge profits. The home mortgage lenders did not care about anything other than the investment banks buying the bundles of mortgages. They would find a way to give anyone a mortgage as long as they had someone to buy the mortgage and take it off their hands. The lending banks rarely held onto the mortgages.

It was this availability of money that drove the price of homes up. The banks were the driving force of prices going up and then were lending more money for people to buy these homes.

One of the problems with this approach to mortgages is that there are only so many people with credit good enough to honestly deserve a mortgage. This did not stop the banks. The profits they were making obviously had a blinding effect and they were unable to see the whole picture.

The credit rating agencies appeared to be more interested in fees than in turning down applications. They kept giving high ratings to bundles of mortgages, much higher than warranted.

When fuel prices went up and adjustable mortgages adjusted up and jobs were lost, what did anyone think would happen? A major problem was the fact that very few people were thinking at all. They were too busy counting their profits. The combined effect was disastrous.

A balloon can hold only so much air and then it bursts and comes down a lot faster than it went up. Mortgage banking was a big balloon. Oil prices provided the pin that burst the mortgage banking balloon. Many people have argued this point with me saying that mortgage policies caused the recession. They did not. Mortgage policies were a house of cards but it was oil prices that provided the wind that knocked them down.

If the mortgage crisis had caused the recession, why didn't the economy rebound when the banks were bailed out in 2009?

When a three hundred thousand dollar mortgage adjusts up from six percent to eight percent, it costs the borrower about four hundred fifty dollars per month additional and most of that is tax deductible. The rise in oil prices cost the borrower about fifteen hundred dollars per month and is not tax deductible. Now let's see. Which one had the bigger effect?

Now combine all this with the fact that the home owner may be seeing reduced income from his job or business. The end result could be deadly to all involved.

Chapter 7

Nobody has yet shown me how American mortgage policies caused Europe to go bankrupt and caused revolutions in the Mideast, but I can show anybody how oil prices caused the worldwide recession and the many ramifications it is having on global stability.

Back to oil prices.

Shortly after hitting a high of one hundred forty seven dollars a barrel in the summer of 2008, oil prices began to plummet. Prices for a barrel of West Texas Crude went straight down to thirty two dollars by the end of 2008 with only a few hiccups on the way down. This was one heck of a roller coaster ride. Where would prices go next?

Please understand that the fact that oil prices dropped so violently over such a short period of time was proof, to my eyes and I believe to anybody who understood anything about the markets, that it was never India or China.

Nothing drastic happened to their economies. They did not close for vacation or go out of business. Nothing significant happened to them. So what was going on? For oil prices to drop so dramatically, they had to have been artificially propped up.

All this talk about economics made me hungry so I went to lunch.

Really, I went to lunch at Gino's, one of my favorite pizzerias in town. I usually go at about one thirty or two o'clock in the afternoon, after the high school kids are gone and I can relax for a few minutes. The local high school is just down the street from me, and the kids have a tendency to overwhelm the food stores for an hour at lunch time. I had my usual eggplant slice. As soon as Mario, the owner, sees me walk in the door, the eggplant slice goes into the oven. Mario's father started the business fifty years ago and now Mario and his brother Luigi, dressed in their red shirts and white pants and aprons, operate the restaurant.

Mario usually greets me with a "How do you feel?" My response is always "With my hands!" It is like our password and countersign. Mario is the chattier brother. Luigi is the strong silent type. He probably couldn't get a word in when Mario was speaking and Mario was usually speaking.

Mario and I often have interesting conversations about anything from local politics to how to fix the world. He refers to it as "venting." Mario is the unofficial mayor of Lynbrook. He collects and disseminates all the local gossip from behind his counter. Occasionally, he gets the stories correct, but correct or not, his versions are always interesting.

On one side of the counter, I noticed a stack of newspapers from a local free press, The Long Island Press.

The cover story was "Crude" about John Mack, "Mack the Knife" and Morgan Stanley manipulating oil prices.

My eyes bugged out of my head. After I read the story it was like hitting the jackpot on a pin ball game. Lights were flashing and all the bells and whistles were going off in my mind. The pizza was very good also.

According to the article, it seems that Morgan Stanley, with CEO John Mack, along with Goldman Sachs and BP (formerly British Petroleum), formed a commodities exchange, the Intercontinental Exchange (ICE) in the year 2000. In 2001 they bought a small London-based petroleum exchange, the International Petroleum Exchange (IPE), and moved it to Atlanta where ICE is based. The next move was to apply to the Bush administration, or should I say the Cheney administration, for "foreign exchange" status. The application was granted, and the ICE was now deemed to be a foreign exchange.

As a foreign exchange, there is almost no American oversight. It is like being a foreign embassy. There were very few laws that applied to it. The IPE left Britain and so there was no longer any British oversight. There was no French, German or Mongolian oversight. Are you getting the picture? To put it simply, there was no oversight.

The article stated that Morgan Stanley owns tankers (they own or control the Heidmar fleet with almost one third of the world's oil tankers), they own refineries, they have more oil in storage than the national strategic reserves, they are the largest factor in the home heating oil wholesale distribution business, they own the exchange the oil is traded on, and they make bets on the exchange. Does anybody see a conflict of interest??? Many of these corporations owned by Morgan Stanley are registered offshore in countries other than the United States.

It appears that before Katrina, gasoline prices were bouncing around in a fifty cent range. A part of that was possibly Morgan Stanley playing. They were probably stealing nickels, lots of nickels but nickels. A nickel a gallon no one would notice. When Katrina occurred and gas prices shot to $3.50 a gallon from $1.75, people paid the price, grudgingly, but they paid it. Morgan Stanley apparently got the idea that it could play for much bigger dollars.

Initially, Morgan started by making bogus predictions as to where it thought oil prices would go. Morgan predicted that oil would go to seventy five dollars by a certain date, and the small speculators pushed the price to seventy five, making Morgan's self-fulfilling prophecy a fact. I am confident that Morgan had placed long bets (an option bet that prices would go up) before each announcement. Many of the speculators jumped whenever Morgan made a prediction. They were herded like sheep. Whenever Morgan made a prediction, the speculators, following their herd mentality, pushed the prices up to Morgan's prediction.

An additional tactic was whenever Morgan wanted to push prices higher, it would make a long bet and then hold its tankers offshore. When the petroleum inventories would come out, they were reported as being low and oil prices would jump up. Morgan would win the long bet and bring the tankers in at the higher price.

Rest assured that Morgan probably had short bets (an option bet that prices would go down) every time it let prices fall.

One of my customers told me that his neighbor was a captain on one of these tankers. The neighbor told him that he was ordered to anchor up off the coast of Indonesia for several weeks at one point waiting until the inventories would come out low and prices went up.

In June of 2011, President Obama released thirty-eight million barrels of oil from the strategic reserves and put them on the market. Oil prices dropped that day from ninety-eight dollars per barrel to ninety. One week later oil prices shot back up from ninety to ninety-eight dollars. I turned on CNBC to see what was going on. Someone was reporting that the inventory numbers came in extremely low and that was driving the price up. It is my understanding that the tankers were held off Indonesia again.

Morgan Stanley just told President Obama who really runs the world.

Why run for President when you can be a commodities trader?!

What a game!!

I do not always believe everything I read to be gospel but the things stated in this article fit the picture. They seemed to answer my questions in a manner that made sense to me. It was time to check things out.

As I mentioned earlier, I am a tennis player. I used to play Friday nights at a tennis party run by Karen, one of my favorite people. About forty people show up and Karen arranges the matches using all of her talents to keep people of various levels in competitive matches. There are lots of personalities to deal with as well. This one won't play with that one and such. Some people have to be reminded that it is a tennis party, not a tournament. Karen has a great handle on the personalities and also puts out the best dinner buffet in tennis. Most of the people are very nice.

Two guys that I was friendly with were Tony and Paul. They worked on Wall Street, though I am not quite sure in what capacity. I talked to them about the article and gave them each a copy. They were not familiar with the situation but said they would ask around and check on things for me.

The following week Tony greeted me as I came in the door. He stepped up to me saying that every word was true. "I found several people who knew all about it." I saw Paul a little later and he confirmed things as well. I was working up a head of steam.

How could all of this be going on with no reaction from the various oversight agencies? Why aren't the oversight agencies there?? I was dumbstruck. With all this flying around in my head, it was difficult for me to focus on a tennis match. I do not think that I played at my best level that evening.

Chapter 8

When I got home after tennis it was past midnight. My mind was spinning. There was no way that I could fall asleep. I just lay in bed with my brain doing cartwheels.

I made copies of the article and handed them out to friends and people I met in the car. Some people found it interesting, some could not grasp the situation, and some said "How could anything handed out by a limo driver be of any significance?" Screw them.

I gave a copy to my friend Pat at one of the MRAC meetings. Pat is in his late seventies and in great shape. He used to be an Olympic wrestler about umpteen years ago and still has a grip like a vise. Now he is very involved with the fisheries as a representative of New York State to the Federal commissions. He was so impressed by the article that he took out a subscription to the newspaper.

The next Tuesday morning I attended a large business networking breakfast hosted by a major news radio station. About five hundred people attended. I find these functions interesting, though they have never been overly profitable for me. It might just be that I enjoy being around people, after spending so much time by myself in the office.

The breakfast was emceed by Steve Newton (not his real name), a reporter for the Wall Street Journal and a popular financial news reporter for the station. As the function ended, I let some of the crowd at the podium dissipate. I approached Mr. Newton and asked him about Morgan and the article. He already knew all this. He confirmed everything in the article to me and added some additional details. I asked him why he never brought this out publicly. After all, if this had ever become public knowledge, the world economy might have been saved.

His answer to my question was very simple. He turned around and started talking to someone else never looking back at me. At first this really jolted me. Here was a knowledgeable Wall Street reporter who could have saved the world but he didn't have the balls to stand up for something this important. It is a concept that I have always had difficulty dealing with.

At what point do people stand up and cry foul? How offensive does an action have to be before someone is willing to say stop? I was aghast. I could not imagine this. I have always had a great deal of respect for people who do the right thing simply because it was the right thing to do. I also lose a lot of respect for those that don't.

Any respect that I had for Steve Newton was gone.

Many years ago, when I was nineteen and in college, I had some decisions to make. They weren't monumental, but to me at that time they were important. An instructor with whom I was friendly reminded me that I was young and had a lot of years of shaving in front of me.

He said "It makes life a lot easier if you can look yourself in the mirror while you shave." I have used this as a guideline for my life ever since.

Don't get me wrong. I am not Mr. Perfect and nobody is nominating me for sainthood. There have been plenty of times that I have looked in the mirror and said "Dummy, you handled that situation wrong!" I try not to make the same mistake twice. It works for me.

How does Mr. Newton look himself in the mirror? I bet his mirror is cracked.

His radio station is my favorite morning station. They wake me up every day, give me the sports and the weather, traffic conditions all over the metropolitan area (I don't really care about the traffic part), news headlines and then he comes on with the financial news. You can imagine what I say back to the radio. His attitude really got to me.

With regard to Mr. Newton, it took me several weeks to calm down. I soon began to realize that, as a Wall Street reporter, if he were to be cut off by the banks, if the banks would no longer feed him stories, he would have to become a pastry chef or a limo driver. There would be no future in Wall Street reporting for him anymore. I am sure that he made a very nice income and could not replace it very easily. He obviously was not going to jeopardize his income merely to save the world economy. That just wasn't important enough. He was probably waiting for something more significant before he would put his butt on the line.

I understood his failure to speak up, but I still lost a great deal of respect for the man. At what point is a situation significant enough for somebody to put himself at risk? How far wrong and how damaging does a situation have to be before someone would be willing to lose his job in order to correct the situation?

Would you be willing to give up your job to save the world economy or would you say "I don't want to get involved. Let someone else do it?"

You have to realize how many other crucial global situations have been affected by the increase in oil prices. Europe is bankrupt, the Mideast is in revolt, terrorism is being funded, and fifteen million American families have lost their homes. I will expand on these later.

If Newton uncovered a terrorist plot to blow up a building, would he report it or be afraid of retaliation?

Chapter 9

At the limo service, Tommy was keeping me busy. A number of people, who I drove around, worked on Wall Street or in related areas. Many of them gave me further corroboration and additional insights. One gentleman was on his way to vacation with his wife. While I was taking them to JFK from Oceanside he told me that he was a day trader working from home. I turned the conversation to Morgan. He knew all about it. "I can see their trades come in. It's obvious. I can tell right away which trades are theirs."

"If it's so obvious, how come none of the oversight agencies can see it?" We were both amazed that no oversight agency was willing to step up to the plate.

One night in the summer of 2009, Tommy called me on the two-way radio. "Turn around and head out to Islip (MacArthur Airport). The plane is landing in forty minutes." MacArthur Airport is about forty miles east of JFK on Long Island and a lot smaller than JFK is. Many people like the airport because it is so small and easy to get around in. I liked it because it was easy in and out and did not have any of the congestion that JFK or LaGuardia had.

When I am told that a plane is landing, it means that the plane is in the process of landing but not on the ground or at the gate yet. It might be in the landing pattern and two hundred miles out. The plane then has to taxi to the terminal and people can file off the plane. Then the people go to pick up their luggage. That can be five minutes or one hour.

I had just started towards LaGuardia when Tommy called. The MacArthur flight had been due in earlier but was delayed in Chicago because of weather. Some of the airlines were very good about posting delays and keeping everyone informed. Some were not. Delta was one of the latter and this flight had caught Tommy by surprise. It was just after rush hour. The weather was clear and traffic was light so I was able to make good time.

I was picking up a Miss Connors and taking her to Battery Park City on Manhattan's lower west side. Many Wall Street people live there because they can walk to work. I actually got to MacArthur a few minutes early and sat for fifteen minutes in the parking lot of the diner located directly across the street from the airport entrance. I left her a message on her cell phone that I was at the airport waiting for her and to call me when she landed. Then I could coordinate picking her up.

Fortunately Miss Connors only had carry-on baggage and she came straight out after she got off the plane.

She was an attractive blond about fortyish. The one hour trip into the city gave us plenty of time for conversation.

She told me that she was an attorney for a law firm on Wall Street. Naturally, I had to ask about Morgan Stanley's manipulation of oil prices.

"It's an open secret. Everybody knows about it." she stated.

"Everybody knows about it? So why isn't anybody doing anything about it?" I asked.

"I have no idea" she replied.

The concept that it was an open secret and no one was speaking up and no agency stopping it was really getting to me. It is probably just another case of "Wall Street Reporter Syndrome." Maybe the law firm is worried that if it was ever found out that someone in their firm had blown the whistle on Morgan Stanley, the major banking firms would pull their business from the firm. It is much easier to let someone else deal with it.

This ate at me for months and still does years later.

I turned my television on to my favorite financial news station, CNBC, but day after day they would talk about all the ups and downs in the economy but never relate it to oil prices. They seemed to cheer the rise in oil prices as they would for the stock price of a major corporation. Does anybody there understand the mechanics of the economy?

There are many good minds at the station. Some of them must know what is going on, yet they never said anything about Morgan Stanley and oil prices.

Then one day I was hit with a dose of reality. It was a really big dose of reality.

I had turned on the station and they were doing a commercial for ICE. Shortly thereafter there were commercials for Morgan Stanley and Goldman Sachs. It is my sincerest belief that CNBC was never going to come out with the truth about oil prices and its effects on the economy because they didn't want to lose the income from the commercials. They would never come out and say that oil and other commodity prices were being manipulated.

Both Morgan and Goldman supplied many interviewees and commentators to the station. I assume that several people at the station had to know the truth but either did not want to say anything or were not permitted to do so. They were just like the radio station reporter only much bigger. There went my respect for the station. How contagious is "Wall Street Reporter Syndrome?"

Chapter 10

I had Dr. Dan in the car again. He was returning from an economic conclave in Indianapolis. Many economists from all over the country spent three days discussing and trying to figure out what happened to the economy. I asked Dan if anyone had mentioned fuel prices. He said no. He had never heard the word mentioned.

"How could they not mention fuel? Fuel is the biggest factor in the economy and the cost of goods. How can it be that they could not relate the cost of fuel to the effects on the economy?"

"I know," he replied, "but I never heard it mentioned." I wanted to ask him why he had not mentioned it, but I think that I already knew the answer. He never thought of it. Even if he had thought of it, I doubt that he would have the balls to stand up and say something different from what everybody else was saying.

Attending this conclave were some of the leading economic minds of our country and they were missing the biggest economic event in our lifetime and maybe longer. I bet many of these attendees were professors like Dr. Dan. What are these people teaching our children? Who pays economists and why?

Wouldn't it be funny if several economists could not attend this conference entitled "What's going wrong with the economy?" because they couldn't afford the gas to get there? They probably would never make the connection. The only trouble was this is no laughing matter.

Maybe next year I could be one of their guest speakers.

Can you imagine Mr. Arrogance himself, the illustrious Dr. Dan, sitting in a seminar and I was the speaker. I can just picture him sitting there with the black shoe polish hair dye dripping down his cheeks, taking in my every word. I would love it.

This is highly unlikely to ever happen but I laugh just picturing it in my mind. Lubricant selling limo drivers are allowed to have a sense of humor, too. How do you think many of us make it through the day?

Chapter 11

Now back to the roller coaster ride of oil prices topping out at one hundred forty seven dollars in the summer of 2008 and then plummeting to thirty two dollars by year's end. As the oil prices climbed to the one hundred forty seven mark, mortgages started to fail all over the country.

It seems that when the mortgage failure rate hit ten and twelve percent, the margin lenders called the investment banks and asked for the other thirty nine billion dollars in cash. Remember when the banks bought a forty billion dollar bundle of mortgages for one billion down? Now they were being asked for the other thirty nine billion in cash.

It is the same as when you buy a stock on margin. If the stock price goes down, you usually get a call from your broker asking for more cash. The difference here is that you are required to put at least fifty percent down and these people are only putting down two and one half percent. That is a big difference, a very big difference.

Naturally the banks did not have that amount sitting around in a drawer, so they suggested that the margin lenders call the insurance companies. The insurance companies, Fannie Mae, Freddie Mac, FHA, AIG, said they had three or four times their normal reserves sitting around in cash just in case of an emergency. However, now they were being asked for one hundred times their reserves. A ten percent failure rate is one hundred times greater than the historic rate of one tenth of one percent. The insurance companies did not have that much cash on hand. They are obligated to cover the losses, but they did not have the cash.

The insurance companies were about to fail as well as the margin lenders and most of the major investment banks. Most of these companies are global in scope, so the whole world was about to experience a colossal collapse of the entire global financial and economic structure. This is when President Obama, shortly after taking office, bailed out the banks and insurance companies. The planning for this bailout started with the Bush administration. This was not a Democratic move nor a Republican move but simply an executive move that had to be done. If Obama didn't act, the situation would have been much worse, and the economic recovery would have taken many years longer.

Among the big banks, Goldman Sachs was the only one relatively unscathed. It predicted the mortgage crisis. After all I did, why shouldn't they? It seems that they sold off their mortgage backed securities to clients while they were shorting them (betting that the securities would lose value) at the same time. In certain circles you are supposed to have the best interests of your clients as top priority. This was supposed to be one of those circles.

Telling your clients to buy something while you are betting it will lose value is considered very unethical. For this conflict of interest the SEC ordered Goldman to pay a five hundred sixty five million dollar fine. That sounds like a lot of money to you and me, but Goldman was earning a profit of one billion two hundred million dollars a month at the time. This fine equated to two weeks profit, not enough to make anyone at Goldman blink. It amounted to little more than pocket lint.

Morgan Stanley, on the other hand, did not see the mortgage collapse coming and it got clobbered. One side of the company was making money on the commodities while the mortgage backed securities side was losing so much that it could have taken the company down. Forty to one leverage is great when you are winning, but it is devastating when you are losing. It could be absolutely deadly.

Morgan Stanley had to stop propping up the oil prices so that prices could drop and homes and mortgages could stabilize. As Morgan stopped propping up the oil prices, the prices started to plummet. This is why oil prices fell from $147 to $32. Once they received their TARP (Toxic Asset Recovery Program) money from the federal government and stabilized their company, Morgan pushed oil prices back up. I am very confident that Morgan had short bets all the way down and long bets all the way back up.

It is interesting to note that the taxpayers had to bailout the same banks which had put the economy into recession in the first place.

Chapter 12

Europe was harder hit than the United States. During this period, oil in Europe was usually ten to twenty dollars more per barrel than in the United States. One hundred dollar plus oil was draining the economies. Greece was the first to be forced into drastic economic cuts. I spoke with several people who said Greece's problems were because of their socialistic economy. Socialism was why their economy was tanking. Nonsense.

The only oil that Greece produced was olive oil and olive oil doesn't get very good mileage inside an engine. The increased cost of the imported petroleum-based oil was draining its economy.

These people could not understand the factor that fuel played in this. I argued that Greece's socialistic policies only made them the first to go with Italy, Ireland and Portugal right behind. We were all sliding down to the edge of the cliff. It was just a question of in what order and how fast we went.

Chapter 13

My high school alumni association has a happy hour get-together once a month. It is usually the first Tuesday of the month, and I help coordinate the event. We never know how many will show up. Sometimes we have four people; sometimes we have forty. On one such evening, I was speaking with an alum who was an attorney representing the banks during this mortgage crisis. He could not accept the fact that oil prices caused the recession. To him, it was caused by the banks giving out money to too many people who did not put down significant deposits.

How did this make Europe go bankrupt? He did not have an answer to my question but still held his position. The investment banks all came out with the same story. They told Congress "The lenders gave out too much money to the wrong people. It is not our fault." Some banks even blamed the people for taking the mortgages. I never heard anyone blame the mortgage brokers. Some of the banks could have said no to people who were not qualified, but why give up those fees and profits?

I find it very interesting that the investment banks which created the recession always had someone else to blame for the problems. The sad part is that so many people who matter always believed the investment banks. I wonder why.

Senator Carl Levin of Michigan was chairing hearings, at the Capitol, on why oil prices were so high and what happened to the mortgage market. The CEOs of all the major investment banks were in front of him and under oath. The banks blamed the speculators for the oil crisis along with India and China and the mortgage lenders for the mortgage crisis.

I called the Senator's office on three occasions during those hearings trying to get to someone who could confront the banks about the manipulation of oil prices. I could not get an aide or anybody to talk with me. The receptionist sounded very interested each time I called. On my third attempt to talk to an aide, I asked her if she was only playing with me because I did not live in Michigan. Between her giggles, she said yes.

Senator Levin was chairing hearings which were of national and global significance, but I could not give him additional information and insight because I did not live in his state. I could not help save the national and global economies because I did not live in Michigan. It was hard for me to believe what had just happened. It was mind-numbing.

I have a lot of respect for my Congresswoman Carolyn McCarthy. After her husband was killed and her son suffered crippling injuries at the hand of a crazed gunman on a commuter train, she didn't quit. She fought back by running for office and trying to help. I think it took a lot of guts on her part to run for office after such a tragedy.

In the early part of 2009 I tried get an appointment with her. It took me four months (the appointment secretary was trying to expedite my appointment) to get a video conference with one of her senior aides. If I was willing to wait another two or three months, I might have been able to speak with the Congresswoman herself.

It was a beautiful June morning when I pulled up to the building where her office was located. I was very hopeful that I could get a member of Congress to hear me out and bring this situation to light in a federal forum. I entered the Congresswoman's office and the receptionist offered me a seat. She had been expecting me. A young man of maybe thirty came out shortly and introduced himself to me and then led me into a conference room. As we entered the conference room an attractive thirty-something young woman appeared on the video screen.

After a minute or two of adjusting the speakers and microphones, our conversation began. We spoke for about forty five minutes. We faxed the aide a number of articles that I had with me, including the Long Island Press article. The young man with me knew of the author of the Long Island Press article and had great respect for him as an investigative reporter. I had very limited knowledge of the reporter's background beyond my recent experiences. Hearing this young man's respect for him gave me a little more confidence. I thought it would help the cause.

I tried to explain to the woman on the video screen how these oil prices were crippling the economy and that Morgan had to be stopped. Her response to me was "Why don't people just pay the higher price?" She could not come close to grasping the concept that taking that much money out of the economy could have such a profound effect. She had no idea that some people did not have the extra money or that the extra money spent on fuel was not being spent in stores. I thanked her for her time. I got up and left.

I thought of calling Senator Chuck Schumer's office but many of the friends that I talked to told me that Schumer's reputation on the street was that he is big banks' best friend. I did not feel like wasting more time.

Who and what is running our government?

Chapter 14

I had lunch with my friend Barbara. We didn't go anywhere special just a local diner. I had to vent some of my frustrations before I went nuts. Some people thought I was already nuts. Barbara looked great and I really appreciated the distraction. Barbara listened intently as I ran on about Morgan, the economy, and McCarthy's aide, but I could see that she was not grasping how all this affected her life.

"Does the high price of gas and heating oil change the amount of money you have to spend?" I asked.

"Yes," she replied.

Then I asked her if she saw any slowdown in her business. She sold insurance. Again she said yes.

"And why is that?"

"Because of the economy," she replied.

I explained, "If you are spending less, then someone else is earning less and they, in turn, are spending less on your products as well as other people's products. Those people earn less and in turn spend less. This is how the spiral works whether in the up direction or in the downward cycle that we are in now." I think she was starting to grasp the picture. She is so sweet and I truly needed someone to vent to occasionally.

The waitress brought our order to the table, and our discussion turned to some of the more social aspects of life.

The various stimulus programs set in play by the Obama administration helped stem the job losses and slow the bleeding but they could not, as I saw it, revive the economy. They just did not reach far enough. Congress made it very tough on Obama to spend on stimulus programs because of the national budget deficit.

You simply cannot create a job unless there is demand for a product or service. There is no demand because no one has any money. To me, this is common sense. Economies all over the world will not improve significantly until oil prices come down. When oil prices come down, you are literally putting hundreds of dollars into almost every household every month. This is far more reaching and more effective than any federal stimulus program could ever be.

Most of the stimulus jobs that were created were construction related as infrastructure was repaired or rebuilt. These people who had jobs because of the stimulus would then spend their paychecks in stores and this would create an upward spiral as the sales would create more jobs in the wholesale, retail, and manufacturing sectors. This is the theory and it can work. On the other hand, if you layoff a lot of people, it feeds the downward spiral and will never turn the economy around. This can't work.

Many right wing Conservatives that I spoke with insisted that all this recession happened because of government being too big. "Reduce the payroll and we will get rid of the deficit and the economy will pick up."

I disagree.

You cannot spur an economy out of recession by laying off several million people. This will only make the situation worse and drive the economy further into the hole. Add to that the fact that these people will receive unemployment compensation for an extended period which will defeat the purpose of laying them off in the first place.

Many people think of the federal government as something less than a high efficiency operation. If we laid off a lot of workers and then paid them unemployment compensation, the government would be getting zero efficiency from these people. The people would be getting paid for no work. This is a concept that the right wing conservatives have yet to grasp.

In good economic times if, you reduced the work force from government jobs, people would have a chance to find jobs in the private sector. A slow reduction of the work force would give people a chance to be absorbed by the private sector. In tight economic times such as we were in then, there was almost no hope of those people finding meaningful employment.

It was interesting to watch high profile analysts interviewed on CNBC. Oil prices were going up and down. When they were headed down for a few months, the additional money spent in the economy started to spur things along. As people paid less for their gasoline, they had dollars left over to spend elsewhere. This additional spending would show up in the next quarterly report of companies. Then oil prices would go up again, and some analyst would be looking at the last three months reports and predict that the economy had turned up and would continue up.

Did he not realize that the spending that spurred the economy had already stopped and things would slow down again? He obviously had no idea what spurs the economy and what slows it. Reading a chart is easy. Understanding the underlying causes for movement on that chart is another story. How much is he getting paid? Does he know Dr. Dan?

When the price of gas at the pump goes down, it does more to spur the economy than any federal program. It literally puts additional spending money directly back into the hands of millions of households around the country. Most of these households do not have extra cash lying around so every dollar gets used. Why can't these analysts understand basic economics? Are they sitting too high in their ivory towers to grasp what is happening on the street below them?

Chapter 15

My conversation with Miss Connors kept bouncing around in my head. Everybody knows about it but nothing is being done about it. I could not sit still any more. I had to try to do something. Finally, I called the SEC. The woman who took my call asked me if Morgan Stanley was doing this manipulation through futures trading. I said probably. She said that was not in her jurisdiction and connected me to the Commodity Futures Trading Commission.

I asked the gentleman from the CFTC if anyone was looking into what was going on. The gentleman from CFTC said that he could not talk to me about anything that might or might not be under investigation and directed me to the CFTC website. I had to fill out the form on the website. That was the only way I could call in a complaint. My frustrations were boiling over, but I bit my lip.

I am willing to bet everything I own that someone had called in a warning about the 9/11 disaster but since he wasn't on a computer, nobody listened to him. It seems you have to be online for anyone to listen to a complaint. Doesn't make any sense to me but then again I am just a lubrication selling limo driver. What do I know?

I kept trying to get someone in the media to help expose this. I tried calling the newspapers, but without proof in their hands, they would not risk the liability of printing anything. If Morgan sued the newspaper, it could be very expensive to defend against without proof to justify their claims. It was much easier for them to look the other way.

Getting this information out to the public was becoming something of a fixation to me. One of my passengers had mentioned the Lou Dobbs' radio show. He said he listened in very often. I was totally unaware of the show at that point. I knew of Mr. Dobbs and had heard him speak at a real estate convention a few years back. So I called in to Lou Dobbs' radio show and actually got on the air.

I was put on the air almost immediately. I guess Mr. Dobbs did not have many calls backed up.

I don't know if I got on the air because my topic was so interesting or because so few other people were calling in. Dobbs said that he agreed with me and then could not get me off the air fast enough. My fifteen seconds were up. His voice said that he seemed nervous with me bringing up such a topic and naming a major bank. I guess that he had a case of "Wall Street Reporter Syndrome."

This was beginning to consume a lot of my conversations with my friends as well as new acquaintances. I would meet women and naturally they would ask "What do you do?" My answer was simple.

"I have a distributorship for automotive and mechanical lubricants and I am trying to save the world economy on the side." Most asked me to explain the "save the world economy" bit but very few were able to understand.

I think I have a good mind and I need that from a companion. Sex is great, but every now and then you want someone to talk to as well. It's great when you can find good sex and a good mind in the same place. If these women could not grasp the concepts I put forward, I guess they weren't for me anyway.

Chapter 16

In November of 2009 I called the British embassy. The Brits were highly affected by the high oil prices and I figured they would be interested in what I had to say. Guess again. The gentleman who answered the phone must have thought that I was a wacko and told me politely to take my problems to the American agencies. The frustrations were building.

In February 2010, the frustrations were getting to me again. I went back to the CFTC. I spoke to the same gentleman that I spoke to six months earlier. I asked him if anybody was looking into what was going on. He replied that he could not discuss anything with me and directed me back to the website. This time I filled out the form and submitted it. At some point I am willing to play the game the only way people were willing to play the game with me.

Two months later, in mid-April, I called him back. I told him that I understood that he could not comment on an ongoing investigation, but I was curious to know if they found anything worth looking into.

"We are receiving a number of calls on the matter now and it is definitely being looked into."

Hallelujah!

The fact that other people were calling in gave me a tremendous lift and that it was actually being looked into gave me a feeling that is hard to describe. There is plenty of room here at the asylum. All are welcome. The scary part came when I realized that I might have been the first to call it in. Who am I?

Two weeks later, on my formerly favorite radio station, I am awakened to the news that "there is a rumor on Wall Street that DOJ (Department of Justice) is looking into Morgan Stanley probably for derivative trading." I loved it!

Oil was at eighty-seven dollars that day, and over the next ten trading days, it dropped to sixty-eight dollars. I called my contact at the CFTC and pointed this out to him. He was almost as pleased as I was. As the initial reaction to the radio announcement ebbed over the next few weeks, oil prices came back up.

Barbara and I had lunch at Gino's. As we came through the door, Mario greeted me with "How do you feel?"

"With my hands," I countered with my hands waving at him. Then he asked Barbara for her order. My eggplant slice went into the oven without my saying a word.

As Barbara and I sat, she asked, "Why are you doing all this work? What's in it for you?"

"I can't be aware of what is going on and just stand around. I can't stand by and watch these people play a rigged version of Monopoly with the world. Morgan devastated my business and many, many others. I have seen businesses and homes lost. How can anybody know what is going on and just sit there? What am I supposed to do? Maybe I should send them a thank you note or a box of chocolates. I could not look myself in the mirror if I didn't try to stop it."

"What if someone tries to stop you? You might get shot."

"I've been shot at before." Her eyes widened at my response. "I was a lieutenant in Viet Nam. In Nam we were fighting for things that affected me less personally than this. These guys are stealing fifteen hundred dollars a month from you, from me and from everybody else, not counting the business we have each lost. Screw 'em!"

"Is there a reward in it for you? Do you get anything for saving the world?"

"Someone told me about the 'Whistle Blower's Law' and I looked into it. It pays whistle blowers a nice chunk of the penalties received from the guilty parties. I understand that it ranges from fifteen to thirty percent of the penalty. If it ever gets to that point the fines could be in the tens of billions of dollars."

"Wow! And you could get a piece of that?"

"I checked with an attorney in Washington and he told me that I did not qualify as a whistle blower because I did not work for Morgan. Maybe I should try to get a job with them." I said jokingly. "Even if I had a job as a doorman, I might qualify."

"This is probably why many of the others who called in bothered to get involved. Money is a great motivator, unfortunately not in my case" I added. Our lunch came and I could see all the "what ifs" rolling around in her mind.

"Barbara," I added, "sometimes you have to do the right thing just because it is the right thing to do. This to me is the right thing to do. I don't think that I could live with myself if I didn't at least try." She nodded in agreement. I hope she understood.

Chapter 17

Congress was busy trying to pass legislation that would prevent the speculators from making trades that might bring down the economy again. How do they know that this was all caused by the loosely regulated speculators? The major banks, Morgan and Goldman, et al, told them so. Congress still doesn't realize that it wasn't the speculators. It was the manipulators. Maybe Congress doesn't want to realize it. The oil companies and the big banks have a lot of friends in high places.

Politicians love those campaign contributions.

Do you know what happens to those campaign contributions if they are not used on a campaign? The politicians keep them. There is a reason why politicians go into politics.

In mid-August of 2010, I called my contact at CFTC. I asked him if the financial regulations that Congress was working on so diligently would affect trading on a foreign exchange, or were we just spitting into the wind and chasing all of our business offshore. He answered in a slightly excited tone that they were discussing that very question in the conference room as we spoke. While he and I were talking on the phone, the powers that be were discussing this issue right down the hall.

"Great" I said "because Morgan and Goldman are trading on the ICE which is a foreign exchange."

"Don't worry about them. We got 'em! It is coming! We got 'em!" I loved the excitement in his voice. This is coming from a man who can't officially say anything to me. I was flying. He was referring to the investigation of Morgan and Goldman. Apparently the CFTC found enough evidence against them for manipulating the commodity prices.

It is hard to put into words what I was feeling. Everything that I have been ranting about for so long had been verified by the CFTC. I was not nearly as crazy as I was beginning to believe I was. It's ok. You can give away my room at the asylum.

No one was buying me dinner but having one finger in saving the world economy really floats my boat. When I shave in the morning, it is real easy to look myself in the mirror. While walking down the street, I had a little extra spring in my step and every now and then for some unexplained reason, there was a grin on my face. I felt great.

In October 2010, Arizona State presented another of its annual awards to the economist who predicted four major indexes for four years in a row and was closer to the actual number than anybody else. The school had changed the date of the award ceremony from December to early

October each year. It seems that the weather was too cold here in New York during December for the school staff who flew in from Arizona. New York City is a little cooler than Phoenix. The school staff did not have wardrobes for a New York winter.

This year's winner was Dr. Cynthia Conklin, (not her real name) an attractive little blonde. (That must be the bachelor in me speaking.) Dr. Conklin's first job after getting her doctorate was as special assistant to Paul Volcker, Chairman of the Federal Reserve for many years and one of the great economic minds of our country. Chairman Volcker attended the ceremony to present the award to Dr. Conklin.

It was interesting to meet Chairman Volcker. He was very cordial to all the guests who asked to take pictures with him. I passed on the photo-op. He is an extremely tall man. At eighty three years of age and slightly stooped, he still stood six foot seven and towered over everybody at the ceremony. Dr. Conklin was somewhat petite and barely came up to his navel.

Dr. Conklin gave a very impressive presentation of her views on the economy as it existed and her predictions for the next year. Her presentation was the most impressive of any I had seen previously. I agreed with ninety-nine percent of what she said, but that one percent clawed at me.

During the question and answer period, someone from the audience had asked her about oil prices. She said that oil prices were high because of India.

"The economic growth in India was demanding more oil and thus driving the prices up and there was nothing we can do about it."

I disagreed with that statement. Actually, it was my understanding that global consumption of oil was down twenty percent from prerecession usage. After her presentation, several people went up to her to offer congratulations. As the line went down, I approached her and Chairman Volcker and offered my congratulations. I said that I agreed with almost everything she said except one item. "What's that?" she scowled at me as her smile vanished.

"It isn't India who is responsible for oil prices going up."

"Who is it? Who is it?" she demanded with a less than cordial sneer on her face.

"It's Morgan and Goldman," I replied.

She looked at Volcker and laughed. "Morgan and Goldman," she said mockingly and walked off with her nose in the air. Volcker looked at me, saying nothing and followed her. I did not pursue the topic with them as I believed that the CFTC would be coming out very soon with an announcement in this regard and that would be more than enough vindication for me.

I had a smile on my face knowing that the CFTC just verified everything I said so I just bit my lip and enjoyed the evening. Something did bother me though. It had me a little unsettled as I thought more about it and the more I thought about it the more unsettling it became.

Now I was becoming really scared. Paul Volcker, one of the greatest economic minds in the world, doesn't know what's going on in what is probably the greatest economic event in our history. If he could not put the pieces of the puzzle together, why should I believe that anyone else would be able to do so? Thank heaven for the other people who called the CFTC or I would feel like the only sane inmate at the asylum. Then again maybe I am nuts and everyone else is sane.

Chapter 18

My new tennis group is a lot of fun. We play three mornings a week at 7:30 AM and I can be back in my office by 9:30. One woman sends out an email asking about your availability to play the following week. You respond and the next day she sends you your matches for the week. Playing this often has improved my game and the exercise is great. Between the tennis and the dancing, my cardiologist was very happy. My orthopedist was getting a little concerned.

When I played golf, I used to play a lot but not for the last few seasons, it takes up the whole day. If I was lucky, I might be back to my office by four in the afternoon.

A number of the members of the tennis group, especially on Saturday mornings, are attorneys. Almost nobody would believe my story about Morgan causing the recession. I mentioned it several times after the CFTC began its investigation. I think some of the players were getting tired of my same old story. When I brought up the subject of Morgan, recently one attorney asked if I was "still on that kick."

My only response: "Absolutely!"

It was now December 2010 and I was starting to get a little concerned that I am not hearing any announcements about Morgan, no whispers or rumors. My friends on Wall Street weren't hearing anything either. I was getting very concerned.

I called the CFTC again and asked my contact, "When is it coming?" His response stopped me cold.

"I don't know what to tell you. There is nothing more I can do. It is up to the bosses. I am sorry but there is nothing that I can do." His voice sounded very depressed. I said thank you and hung up. If I thought he sounded depressed, it was nothing compared to the voices in my head.

It took a little digging on my part but I figured out that the Commissioner of the CFTC, George Richardson, (not his real name) was a former Goldman Sachs partner, and most probably, he quashed the investigation. I doubt that he would indict his friends. How did he ever get this position of oversight of his friends? Wouldn't his resume shout "conflict of interest?" I do not think that anyone will ever give me an answer to that question, so I never bothered to ask anyone.

The CFTC also has an Environmental and Energy Advisory Board upon which sit representatives from Goldman, Morgan, J.P. Morgan and Merrill Lynch as well as a representative from my favorite foreign exchange, the ICE. Why is a foreign exchange (ICE) sitting on the United States Commodity Futures Trading Commission? I think this is a very good question and someday I hope to ask someone. That is if I ever get to talk to someone.

I can just imagine the DOJ putting its findings on the table at a CFTC meeting and these people looking at one another and saying "Nah, we don't feel like indicting ourselves this morning." End of discussion.

It took me a little while to calm down enough to think rationally again. After all, I just came from a mountainous high to a cavernous low in nothing flat. I think that when I hit the bottom, I may have bounced a few times. I came down so fast that I am surprised that I did not get the bends.

The concept that the Commissioner of the oversight agency, being fully aware of the goings on, would allow this to continue was a concept that I was not ready for. The fact that he was duplicitous in allowing this to go on was too much for me to comprehend. I would give everything I own to be in the room when someone tells him to turn around and put his hands behind his back as they slap the handcuffs on him.

I pray that day comes soon.

Understand that we are not talking about a building commissioner approving a zoning variance so that a friendly developer could build what otherwise could not be built or to speed up the approval process. We are talking about something that has destabilized the world as we know it. Europe is bankrupt, the Mid-East is in revolt, terrorism is being funded, and fifteen million American families have lost their homes. People have been driven to homicide and suicide. Yes, these increases in oil prices have done all this and more. It is my opinion that Morgan Stanley has done more damage to the American economy than all of our enemies combined. Now add all the damage done to the rest of the world.

It would be impossible to quantify the total damage done to the world economy by putting a monetary number on it. The number would be too high to comprehend. The term "trillions" would be de minimus.

Chapter 19

In January of 2011, Egyptians began to revolt against the Mubarak regime, and yes, I can show the direct connection from oil prices to the Egyptian revolt.

It seems that forty percent of Egypt lives on two dollars a day. The Egyptian blue collar workers did not participate in the profits of the increased oil prices, but their expenses went up. Evidently they do not have the same union structure as we have here in America. The increased price of wheat on the global markets may have had a significant effect on the Egyptian workers.

They had a twenty percent increase in the cost of food and a fourteen percent increase in the overall cost of living. The rise in fuel prices drove up their cost of food and other necessities. How could anyone ever expect them to absorb that on two dollars a day?

This had nothing to do with the American mortgage debacle and to date nobody has been able to show me any connection between the Egyptian revolt and the mortgage fiasco. Please note that the American banks were bailed out in 2009.

I have often used the saying that fat people do not go to war but hungry people do. Fat people have everything they want, but hungry people, on the other hand, will fight to feed their families. They will follow anyone who will help put food on the table. To what extremes would you go if you could not feed your family? What would you do if your child was crying for food and you had none to give? Would you go on welfare? What if there was no welfare system to help your family? Would you rob a store? What would you do?

The Muslim Brotherhood stepped in and told the hungry Egyptians "Follow us and we will get you food and everything you need." They overthrew Mubarak with the populace support.

This has happened many times throughout history. Adolf Hitler rose to power because after World War One, Germany was left bankrupt, and its people were cold and hungry. The German people were forced to pay for France and England's war expenses. Their country was left bankrupt. The German populace was willing to follow anyone who could turn their economy around and put food on the table. They picked a maniac.

The United States learned an important lesson after World War One. After World War Two ended, the U.S. rebuilt Germany and Japan and supplied their citizens with food and coal, so that this situation would not happen again. We helped rebuild their industries so that their economies could function and the countries could become self-supportive again. We rebuilt them so well that they became economic powers. Apparently we learned our lessons, but sometimes we have to learn them the hard way.

Currently, there is a civil war in Syria for much of the same reason as Egypt had. The Muslim Brotherhood now controls Egypt and will soon control Syria. At the moment, they are saying that they have no intention of attacking Israel or cutting off oil supplies to the non-Muslim countries. These intentions could change tomorrow.

Some of the other Mid-East oil producing countries have decided to share a piece of the profits with their people and pay out a sort of social security payment to each family. That way the people will have no reason to revolt. This seems to be working.

The Muslim Brotherhood is now a major player in the Mid-East and a factor in global stability. They might have access to nuclear weapons and missiles. What their next move is or what position they will take on an issue in the future is anyone's guess.

Chapter 20

I stopped down at the marina where I used to keep my boat. My boat was a twenty five foot center console, ideally set up for the guys going fishing. It was a little short on creature comforts for women as it did not have a cabin. Any woman fishing with me needed a strong bladder. Fishing on my boat was a passion, but when the economy went south, I found myself working too many hours to use it and the money I was spending on annual maintenance and dockage was better spent on things like rent and food.

Fuel prices at the dock are always higher than the local gas stations where you might take your car. Prices hit five and a half dollars per gallon and boats use a lot of gallons. In a car you can always drive to another gas station. There is usually another one within a few blocks if not across the street. You can't drive your boat a few blocks inland for cheaper fuel. On the water there aren't many options.

Anyway, I got into a conversation with Pete, the marina owner, and his son about the economy and Morgan. (It seemed that I mentioned Morgan wherever I went.) Pete used some of my products on his yard equipment. Pete's had vacancies at his marina which is something I had not seen in the fifteen years that I kept my boat there. Pete was impressed with the information I had. He suggested that I speak to Charlie, a friend of his, who owned fifteen local town newspapers, who might be able to help me.

I really wanted to get this information out to the public. That is the only way I could see any of these politicians reacting. This seemed like a great opportunity to me. I really thought that this was an opportunity worth checking out.

I called Charlie (not his real name) the next day, and after a short but cordial conversation, he asked me to write an article for his papers. I did. My first article was twenty-five hundred words. Charlie went berserk.

"I wanted one hundred twenty five to one hundred fifty words. Not a novel," he screamed. It would have been great if he had told me that earlier. I never met Charlie, but he seemed to be elderly and slipping just slightly. I wrote a shorter article which he published but nothing ever happened. He did, however, have a local cable TV show with Governor Cuomo every week. If I could get to speak face to face with the Governor, it would be great even if it was for only a minute or two. It might be my opportunity to make something happen.

I asked Charlie to get me a two minute sit down with the Governor. He said that he would try, but it was up to the Governor's appointment secretary. Charlie kept forgetting about asking and then could not remember who I was so I gave up.

Chapter 21

I spent most of 2011 trying to find another federal agency to report that a federal commissioner had just quashed an investigation. If that investigation had ever come to light, it would have turned the entire world economy around. It should be fairly easy or so I would imagine. A commissioner who may have committed a crime with major global implications should be of interest to somebody. Guess again.

How much would an investment bank like Morgan or Goldman be willing to compensate a commissioner like Richardson to allow them to get away with what they were doing? How much would it be worth to them? Mind you that I have absolutely no knowledge that anyone was paid off but it is great mental fun just trying to put a value on what a payoff might be. The number might be staggering. A payoff could come in the form of cash or stock or inside information about an unrelated investment or some future quid pro quo.

How much would you be willing to pay off a government official to allow you to make billions and billions of dollars? Maybe it was just done out of friendship, maybe not.

My first call about this issue was to the U.S. Attorney General's office in Washington, D.C. I figured that the AG's would be interested in what amounts to, in my opinion, criminal behavior by the commissioner of a watchdog agency. A very pleasant sounding woman politely directed me to the FBI. She had no interest in anything I had to say.

I called the FBI. The receptionist passed me right through to the duty officer. We spoke for quite a few minutes, maybe fifteen or twenty. He genuinely seemed interested, made notes and took all my contact information. Did anybody call you? Nobody called me. I called the FBI three times with almost identical results each time, but each time the call was shorter in duration.

It was tough for me to accept that nobody from the FBI would call me back. Could it be that this was just not significant enough?

I emailed the President. Why not aim high? I received back a very polite automated response thanking me for my email and informing me that the White House receives over six thousand emails a day and could not possibly read all of them. I doubt that they read any of them. Nobody ever called back. I emailed the White House three more times with the exact same result. At least these folks are consistent.

I noticed an article in my local newspaper about the Building Trades Association meeting with local and state politicians to try to get construction going again in order to create work for their members. If I could talk to someone in the Association, maybe he could help me get to these politicians. If the politicians could help me get the word out, it would be a major benefit for the Association and their members. I doubt if they would mind if it helped the rest of the world at the same time.

I called and asked for the president of the Association as his name was the only one mentioned in the article. The woman who answered the telephone did not know what to make of my story and told me, "I am sorry but he is much too busy to take your call." She politely excused herself and hung up. I called back several weeks later with similar results.

The next time that I redo my home, please remind me to put up padded wallpaper. I have been knocking my head against the wall so much lately that I am surprised that I have any walls left. I am surprised that I have a head left.

Chapter 22

Finally, I took some time off. I needed it. I went to Los Angeles to see my favorite goddaughter in the whole world, Hallie. Her mother, Margo, is technically a third cousin to me, but functionally she is more like a cross between a sister and a daughter. Hallie's father, Andrew, and I get along like brothers. It was Hallie's graduation from high school, an event I could not miss. Since I don't have any children myself, Hallie fills a very big gap in my life and since she doesn't have any uncles or close relatives, I hope that I fill a gap in her life. She is also my favorite photographic subject. Her home is my gallery. There are over seventy of my photos hanging in their house, mostly of her.

While we were out having dinner with some of their close friends, someone suggested that I make a video and set up a blog to espouse my thoughts of Morgan and the oil crisis. He thought we could make a lot of money by charging people a monthly membership to the blog. The idea of the video intrigued me. I had not thought of it before. Making money interests me too, but it was not my driving force. Apparently it was his. My concern was to get the message out to the public. Let public outrage force the oversight agencies and politicians to act.

When I got back to New York, I found a friend's son who had an old-fashioned video camera. We set it up in my living room. I even put on a jacket and tie for the occasion. Working from home, I rarely wore a tie. When I worked in the city, a suit and tie was the uniform. Working from home, jeans and a tee shirt are the official dress code. I used to buy four or five new suits every year because I would wear them out. In the twenty-five years that I have been working from home, I have not bought five suits in total. The video was about twenty minutes long. My friend Danny is a bit of a computer geek and helped me get it on You Tube. Because of the length of the video, we had to break it into Part One and Part Two. I was psyched.

The first hit on the video gave me a rave review. I passed the video link to everybody I could think of. I am a dancer, hustle, lindy, cha-cha and such. Every Tuesday evening I join a group of friends at a local restaurant with a band and a dance floor. Most of us have been dancing together for several years. I grabbed every email address that I could and sent out the link to my video. I called customers and sent them the link. I was ready for this to go viral.

It didn't. Some people came back to me with great reviews. For many it was over their heads. They all were being affected by the high oil prices and the recession, but

I guess they just could not connect the dots. I had about one hundred fifty hits to Part One and seventy hits to Part Two. I wonder how many of those hits were me checking to see how many hits I had. It definitely was not viral. Heck it wasn't even a sneeze. I guess that I did not have enough naked women on it or a dog doing stupid tricks.

While attending one of the seminars at a sport fishing trade show, where my club maintained a booth, I met a Newsday reporter. Newsday is the major newspaper on Long Island. It is not the New York Times or Wall Street Journal. Newsday has some global news and some national news, but its main focus is Long Island.

The reporter was very interested in my story. I cautioned him that the newspaper might be more concerned with any potential liabilities connected to running the story than saving the world. After checking with his editor, he got back to me that I was right and they could not run the story without proof that would stand up in court. He referred me to a friend, Jeff, in Washington, D.C. who wrote in some papers that I was not aware of. Jeff told me that he had written about Morgan several times without any response. He did not have any time to talk and had to run to a meeting. End of discussion.

Chapter 23

I called the New York State Attorney General's office in the summer of 2011. Hey, Morgan and Goldman are New York based and much of their trading activity happened from New York. The gentleman who answered the phone referred me to the Buffalo office. He said they were working on something similar. I scratched my head. Buffalo is a long way from Wall Street. Buffalo just didn't seem like the Mecca for something of this nature to me, but he worked in the AG's office so he must have known what he was talking about.

    A very nice woman in the Buffalo office referred me to the Mineola office. It was closer to me. Apparently she did not realize that she was reportedly working on something similar. The woman in charge of the Mineola office told me in a very matter of fact manner "Send me a letter or I can't talk to you!" What was going on? She wouldn't even let me mention what my complaint was about. Nobody would talk to anybody any more. So what if it was the most important situation in the world.

Do you think that Islamic terrorism is more important? Where do you think their funding comes from?

My frustration level was at a boil. I figured that steam must have been coming out of my ears by now.

My high school alma mater holds a career day every year. It was started by the students several years ago. The students were deciding on career fields, but many had never talked to anyone actually in that field. They wanted to be doctors, lawyers and Indian chiefs but had never talked to a real doctor or lawyer about it. On one Saturday morning each year about one hundred alums come in from all over the area representing many different careers. Each sets up in a classroom. The students are given a list of who and what field is in each room and get a chance to converse. The students get an opportunity to talk to doctors, lawyers, engineers, scientists, businessmen, and civil service workers.

Afterwards there is a luncheon for the alums. At the luncheon I met a fellow alumnus who worked for the Joint Terrorism Task Force (JTTF). With sandwich in hand, I asked him if when oil prices were forty dollars a barrel, did petro dollars help to fund terrorism?

"Of course." he responded.

"Does the increase in oil prices make more money available to the terrorists?"

"Absolutely!"

If I can figure this out, why can't somebody who matters figure this out? Do they know what's going on and not care? Everybody can't be crooked or am I just being naïve again? I consider myself to be bright, but there are many people smarter than I. Where are they?

If anyone thinks this is just a case of a few people making some extra money trading, they are being very naïve. I ran into a cousin at a family function recently. He has had a very successful career in the financial arena. I asked him about his thoughts regarding Morgan's activities. He told me there has always been corruption and that I should just learn to go with it.

Sorry, but that is not my style. Maybe that is why I am not rich.

The issue for me at this point was to get this information out to the public. I had to get someone in power to act. My frustration level hovers between high and boiling over. I am thankful for the distractions that tennis, fishing and dancing provide me. I would probably go nuts just thinking about all the people and entities that I have contacted who have the ability to save the world economy and won't. Maybe I am nuts already. The nice thing about being nuts is that you are generally the only person not to know about it. That being said, if I know that I am nuts, does that mean that I am not nuts? I guess that this is something for the philosophers to ponder while I go hit my head against the wall.

I emailed the White House again and son of a gun, I received the same automated response again. After my next attempt to contact someone by email, I spoke with one of the telephone operators who field the calls to the White House. This woman was very nice and seemed to understand some of my frustrations. Understand that these operators just field calls from the public and probably do not handle calls that actually go to people in the White House.

She probably isn't even on the White House grounds. I almost expected the operators to be outsourced to India. She suggested that I fax a letter to the White House and maybe someone might actually read it. Somebody has to pick up the piece of paper before they can throw it away. Sounds like a plan.

I have faxed the White House four times. No response.

Can you imagine what the fallout would be like if it ever came out that the White House operators were in fact outsourced to India? I am sure that they are not, but it's funny to me just thinking about it. There is nothing wrong with a little humor here at the asylum.

I am continually amazed at the number of people who I talk to who cannot accept my theories. They do not have a theory of their own, but how can anything coming from me be right? After all, who am I?

I ran into the mayor of my town at the coffee shop one morning. He is a nice guy but he could not accept my explanation of why his sales tax revenues were down. He had viewed my video previously, but apparently could not grasp what I was saying.

"It's not that" he told me.

"Then what is it?" I asked. He was in the coffee shop but obviously could not smell the coffee brewing.

"I don't know. It is many other factors."

"Yeah, like what?" He did not hang around long enough to discuss the issue. Just like a politician. If you do not have an answer, just keep moving.

Chapter 24

On September 17th, 2011, a rally started in the Wall Street area with people protesting all the financial greed and corruption on Wall Street. Hundreds of people camped out at Zuccotti Park in the heart of Wall Street. It was dubbed "Occupy Wall Street." They seemed to be protesting that some people were making more money than they were. They were receiving media attention from all over the world. They were hoisting signs stating "Wall Street is greedy." They were so close to the target but slightly amiss. I had to go down there and talk to the organizers. If they would only hoist a sign saying "Morgan Stanley is manipulating the oil prices," they could hit a home run and then some.

I have no objection to someone making a lot of money. I respect them and try to learn from them. I do not respect people who would destroy the world as we know it, throw millions of American families out of their homes, cut school programs throughout the country, fund terrorism around the world, cause revolutions and instability in the Mid-East and the list could go on. There are lines in life. How far over the line is acceptable in the name of profits? Don't these people ever look in the mirror when they shave? What do they say to themselves? "Hey, I am a man. I just threw a thousand families out of their homes this week and funded a little terrorism."

I strongly doubt that any of the people involved with the manipulation of commodity prices ever wore a uniform in defense of this country. It would be too oxymoronic to fight for your country in the field then come home and destroy it from your desk.

On Saturday I went to Zuccotti Park. It was quite a scene and a big tourist attraction. It looked like a hippie commune from the 60's. There were tents and sleeping bags all over. The weather was great. I was glad for the demonstrators. Camping out and demonstrating in the rain would not be as much fun or be nearly as effective. What good could the demonstration do if nobody came out to see it?

I kept trying to find the organizers of the Occupy Wall Street movement but people kept deflecting me saying that the leaders were too busy to be disturbed. I wanted to say that we have something in common. I was somewhat disturbed myself. Some people who knew me well might be thinking that I was very disturbed.

However, I did meet some reporters. One in particular was with the New York Times. We spoke again several days later and I emailed him my video. He responded that he was impressed with the video but his editor was afraid of a lawsuit from the banks. If the banks sued, it would be much too costly for the paper to defend. I knew what the response would be before he ever spoke to his editor.

Chapter 25

I attended another Marine Resources Advisory Council meeting. I rarely miss any of them. The reporter from Newsday, the Long Island newspaper, was there. He was a nice guy and apparently respected my efforts. The fisheries are an important business sector on Long Island and he was a business reporter. I told him of my frustrations in trying to get anybody to write about the Morgan situation. If I could only get a copy of the investigation, it would solve a lot of my problems. He made me aware of the Freedom of Information Act, FOIA to its friends. My eyes opened. "It might take you a year but you could get a copy. They have to respond." I was reenergized.

I looked up FOIA on the internet when I got home. It gave me some understanding of the law. Since the CFTC does not have a police force, the Department of Justice most probably ran the investigation. Their investigative arm is the FBI. I called the contact listed on the DOJ website. She was very pleasant and explained to me how to use the FOIA option on the website. I filed a FOIA request. DOJ had twenty days to respond to my request. After nineteen days, I received an email from DOJ asking which of their ninety-seven offices conducted the investigation. How would I know?

I called the contact phone number again and asked which office would handle an investigation requested by the CFTC which is located in Washington, D.C. I had to make a formal response to their response. I responded that it was probably the Washington, D.C. office. They responded to my response that the twenty days were up and I had to file another request and start all over. This went back and forth for five or six rounds. I gave up on the DOJ.

I went to the FBI next. I wound up calling the FBI three times to report that a commissioner had quashed an investigation and but I never received a reply. I rationalized that the phone messages landed on the desk of the people who had done the initial investigation for the CFTC. They probably said to themselves that the investigation was sitting in a drawer and nobody wanted it, so we are not doing it again.

My FOIA requests kept coming back, stating that they could not locate any such file. To hide a file from a FOIA request or to keep anybody else from finding it is very simple. All you have to do is misfile it. Let's say it should be filed under M for Morgan 2010 and somebody "accidentally" files it under R for Russian spies from the 1950's. It may never be found and if years later somebody accidently comes across the file, it would be very easy to blame a low wage file clerk for the error.

My frustration level was skyrocketing at this point. More and more people were beginning to look at me a little sideways. Either they were thinking that I was a little nuts or they were saying "I told you so." Every now and then I started believing that they may be right. Then I would come up with a new approach to attack. I would grab my lance, mount my steed and charge. I think the windmills were getting larger.

Some people kept telling me that there is nothing you can do. Just accept it. It was too big and too many people were being paid off. Politicians like their money and campaign contributions but they like their jobs better. If the populace knew of Morgan's goings on and started to speak out, I believe the politicians would have expressed their outrage and done something. I do not think they will do anything until that happened. In my eyes, nothing in the world was more important, than stopping this global manipulation of commodities.

If you do not believe that this directly affects your life, think again. Fifteen million American families have lost their homes. Europe was going bankrupt. The Middle East was in revolt and the Muslim Brotherhood was becoming its dominant political power. Israel's security was threatened and greater amounts of funding were going towards terrorism. The pinnacle of job security (civil service) was threatened with every city, state, county, and village cutting back on spending and laying off workers, and businesses laying people off to stay alive. Nobody was unaffected. Whatever product you manufacture, sell or service, how would it do in a better economy?

Doctors told me that they were seeing the same amount of patients as they did in good times except that many of the patients they were seeing now had no insurance and could not afford to pay personally. Laid off people very often have no insurance benefits. The hospitals have a legal obligation to treat people whether they can pay or not. Hospital budgets were stretched. Schools were cutting programs. Your kids were not getting the same education and their health and safety were compromised.

In 2012, I attended two commercial fishing trade shows, one in Maine and the other in Massachusetts, trying to sell my products. Cape Cod in January is great. You can get any spot on the beach you want especially if you do not mind the twelve degree temperature. Rockport, Maine in February isn't much different. You could get almost any tee time you wanted on the golf course. Bring the pink balls. They show up better in the snow.

Both trade shows were productive for me businesswise, which was the reason I went in the first place. Having never been to either show before, I decided not to take a booth and just walk around introducing myself and my products as best I could. I thought it a little more prudent to see what was going on before I invested in a booth. I liked the shows and even booked a booth for my business for next year.

One seminar I attended was about the status of the lobster industry and possible new marketing approaches. Of course I mentioned Morgan. If Morgan's stranglehold was broken, demand for the products would probably rise twenty percent here in the United States alone plus the cost of harvesting lobsters and other species would be cut drastically. Fuel prices would drop from four dollars a gallon to two. Fuel is the major expense for offshore fishermen. A gentleman sitting two rows from me agreed strongly.

As the seminar finished, I approached the woman leading the discussion to talk with her. She told me afterward that everything I was saying was over her head. At least she was honest enough to admit it.

Talking with the gentleman who had agreed with me after the session broke, I found out that he was a former congressman and is now a state legislator in Maine. He recommended that I call Elizabeth Warren, Senator from Massachusetts, because she was really into things like this. I have three calls into her, but again I do not live in Massachusetts so I could not get past the receptionist. The receptionist was very polite and probably tossed my name and phone number into the circular file under his desk. Several months later, I received an email from the good senator thanking me for contacting her office. Imagine what I would get if I could actually talk to someone meaningful.

A month or two after the Maine show I contacted the Maine Lobster Promotion Council. You have to understand that fishing and the harvesting of lobsters and other shellfish is a major industry in Maine. In fact, fishing is the number two industry in Maine with lumber being the number one and tourism is number three. Lobster is eighty-five percent of number two and a big chunk of number three. It is a major factor in Maine's economics. The state is dependent upon it. There are only one million three hundred thousand people in Maine, most of whom live near the coast. The success of this industry affects virtually everybody in the state.

No matter what price the fisherman receives at the dock for his catch, lobster is always the most expensive item on the menu of any restaurant. With the recession, fewer people go out to eat as often and when they do, many opt for less expensive items. If I could increase the demand for Maine's products and significantly cut the cost of harvesting, it would greatly benefit them and the rest of the world. All I needed was for one of their congressmen or senators to listen to me for two minutes. Hence, my call to the Promotion Council.

Maggie who answered the phone was very polite and listened to a bit of my rant. I asked her to help me get in touch with one of the legislators with whom the Council has contact. I think she thought that I was a crack pot. "I'm sorry but I don't think we can help you."

I sincerely believe that most people are afraid to make a decision. This is in general and not specific to my situation. Their concern is what if I made a bad decision, then I would be at fault. It is safer for them not to decide but instead pass the buck to someone else rather than risk the embarrassment of making a wrong decision. The Army taught me in Officer Training that it is better to make the wrong decision than to make no decision. In a combat situation, not making a timely decision and worrying about what choice to make generally costs the lives of your men.

Chapter 26

In February 2012, I attended another MRAC meeting. There are seven of them a year. During a break in the action, I was talking with my friend Pat who has been very interested and supportive of my campaign against Morgan. One of the councilors, Ted Caruso (not his real name), was walking towards us.

"Hey, Ted, don't you work for Morgan Stanley?"

"Yeah."

"Aren't you a stock broker?"

"No. I'm a trader. Futures trader. Commodity Futures."

"Really. I understand that George Richardson quashed the investigation by the CFTC?"

"Absolutely! Richardson quashed it." Pat was standing next to me with his jaw hanging open. Ted had no idea what he was admitting to.

"Richardson quashed it?" I repeated back to him.

"Absolutely" he repeated.

"When is it enough for you guys?" I asked, looking him straight in the eye.

"What are you talking about?" He moved closer to me with a quizzical look on his face.

"Europe is bankrupt. The Middle East is in revolt. Fifteen million American families have lost their homes. When is it enough for you guys? You're here trying to save a fish? Where are your priorities?" He turned and ran away from me with tears in his eyes, covering his face, never to look in my direction again. He just confirmed everything that I had been saying for the last six years.

I didn't say anything at the time, but everyone in that meeting room was significantly affected by the actions of Ted and his cronies. Many of the people at the meeting were commercial fishermen or party and charter boat operators. Fuel was their major expense and the recession reduced the amount of their incomes by considerable margins.

Doubling your expenses and reducing your income is not the highlight of a good business plan. Yet, this is exactly what was happening to the people who fish for a living. The party and charter boat operators saw significantly reduced ridership. Many recreational fishermen had reduced the number of times they went fishing. It is not a cheap hobby for many participants. Commercial fishermen received a lower price for their catch.

Could you imagine what would happen if they realized that a major cause of the problem was sitting across the room from them? What if they realized that Ted was responsible for cutting a significant portion of their incomes?

Many of the other attendees were with the Department of Environmental Conservation or other related agencies. The State had cut programs and budgets had been slashed. Programs like reef building (fish need someplace to live and manmade reefs help provide habitat for many species) and the hiring of more environmental conservation officers were scrapped.

I do not believe that anyone other than Pat and I knew that Ted had a hand in bringing on the recession and driving fuel prices up. If they did know, I believe that they would not drag him out back. They would probably just have filleted him right there on the conference room table.

There were so many feelings going on inside me at the same time. I was angry. I was vengeful. I was elated. I was depressed. I was relieved. I felt justified. Pat and I just looked at one another. There was nothing to say.

A week later, with my frustrations boiling over and nowhere to turn, I called the New York State Attorney General's office again. I learned long ago while doing sales to recall offices every so often because the person who wasn't interested before may be interested now or the situation may have changed or you may reach someone else who is interested in what you have to offer.

This time the gentleman who answered the phone was very interested. He told me that I would have to fill out their forms and he would get them out to me right away. It would take two or three weeks for someone to respond to me. I could live with that. Two days later I had the forms in my hand. Naturally I wasted no time in filling them out. I wrote two full pages of small print. In the last line I said that, in addition to the criminal charges, New York might be able to seek damages in the amount of every dollar that New Yorkers spent on fuel over and above a fair price since Katrina. I had to put something in there to keep New York State interested. Money always helps.

The amount of damages could be in the hundreds of billions of dollars. I doubt that New York could ever recover that much but twenty, forty or sixty billion was possible. In addition, New York's expenses would drop and the sales and income tax revenues would increase. How much fuel does the State buy to serve all its vehicles and equipment? New York's whole budget for that year was one hundred thirty eight billion. Would twenty or forty billion dollars have helped cover the cost of the investigation and trial? I think so.

After three weeks I had not heard from anyone, so I called. It was still in process. A week later I received a letter from an attorney in the AG's office telling me that my complaint was forwarded to the antitrust unit of the office. I called the attorney who signed the letter and we had a brief but nice conversation. His job was to sort the wheat from the chaff. In other words, he sorted out the complaints that appeared to be significant and within the auspices of the AG's office and passed them to the proper department. He seemed genuinely excited by my complaint. Apparently it was more than what he typically reviewed.

"You didn't get our 'thank you but no thank you' letter. You should hear something within a few weeks." I was pumped.

One month later I still had not heard anything, so again I called asking for the antitrust unit. The woman answering the phone gave me the name of the attorney my complaint had been referred to but she was not in that day. I left a message and to my surprise, the attorney returned my call early the next morning. We had a brief but friendly conversation. It seemed her boss had told her to contact me. I offered to come to their office, but she said that was not necessary yet and we arranged a conference call for Thursday morning at eleven o'clock, two days later.

Thursday at eleven o'clock sharp, my phone rang. It was the attorney and her boss. I went through some of the history with my complaint but I explained that I could not say that I ever saw someone make a trade. I explained what was going on and some of how it was going on, but my inside knowledge was very limited. This, I believe, is the biggest economic crime in history. This has caused Europe to go bankrupt and Egyptians to revolt and millions of Americans to lose their homes. I explained how the oil prices affected homes, Europe and the Egyptians. The senior attorney said "You sell lubricants for a living??!!"

I spoke of the conversations with my contact at the CFTC and the investigation being quashed by Richardson and that an acquaintance, Ted, at the MRAC, who happened to be a trader at Morgan Stanley, confirmed this to me in front of witnesses.

"Do you think that Ted would be willing to cooperate with us?" they asked.

"That depends on how you approach him," I replied.

"How would you suggest that we approach him?"

"It is very simple. You tell him that he has two options. Option one is to cooperate with the investigation. He can receive immunity and spend the next several years fishing, golfing and having dinner with his family. Option two is to become subject of the investigation and if there is any wrongdoing found, there might be jail time involved, a recapture of any proceeds improperly attained and a forfeiture of any assets purchased with those proceeds such as a house, car or boat, and his family can see him on visiting day. I believe he will cooperate."

I related my adventures in trying to get a FOIA copy of the investigation.

"If you can get a copy of the CFTC investigation, it is a done deal." The attorneys told me that this investigation had already started in their office. Apparently some of the people who had called in to the CFTC after me had called here before I did. I gathered from some of the questions posed to me that the investigation has included a number of additional banks and many different commodities. With no oversight by any agency, commissioners looking the other way and apparent immunity for everyone, it had become a free for all.

I had assumed this for a while and discussed it with the parent company who manufactures my products. I used to sell a one hundred seventy five ounce container of oil additive for one hundred forty dollars and now I sell a one hundred forty ounce container for one hundred eighty five dollars. About three dollars of that increase is from oil prices. The rest is due to the price increases of all the elements that go into it.

Judging from the looks I got from him when he did look at me, my "former friend" Ted at the MRAC is apparently cooperating with the AG's office. He probably does not realize yet that I may have kept him out of jail with many of his assets intact. Someday I hope to remind him of that. Right now I think he hates my guts, and I love every minute of it. He should not go to jail. He should be dragged out back and shot. Fortunately for him I have not touched a weapon since I came home from Viet Nam.

I understand that Ted has told a few people at the MRAC that I turned him in to the AG's office. I wonder if he told them why. I have not discussed his activities at Morgan with anyone other than Pat.

The AG's office will not speak to me nor should they. I can't get any updates. It would be improper for them to give me any information before it is publicly announced. I would love to know if a case is going forward or not. It is hard for me to just sit around and hope for the best. I would love to know everything that is happening in that office. I guess that I will have to learn to live with the fact that they will not confide in me.

Chapter 27

Spring of 2012 saw the King of Saudi Arabia announce that the world could not afford one hundred dollar oil. He said that Saudi Arabia was pumping ten million barrels a day and had eighty million barrels in reserve in case of any interruption. He proclaimed that oil prices were too high. The King of Saudi Arabia actually said that oil prices were too high! The stock market reacted right away. Oil prices dropped to the seventy six to seventy seven dollar range.

Morgan apparently enjoyed this by making its long bets and pushing the prices back up to the one hundred dollar range. How do they keep all those egos within the confines of their offices? Concrete and steel can only hold so much.

Can you imagine that the King of Saudi Arabia was saying that he wanted to make less money for the sake of the world? Saudi Arabia?!?! Morgan still did not have enough.

Actually the King was speaking for the sake of Saudi Arabia and other Middle East oil producers, but it sounded good.

The Saudis knew that, at the higher prices, drilling for new oil sources was happening all over North America and other areas. As it turned out, many new sources of oil have been found in North America making the Middle East's oil supply much less significant. The only problem was that it costs fifty to eighty dollars a barrel to bring the new oil out of the ground depending on where it was.

Russia had found new oil sources but the Russians needed seventy dollars a barrel to bring it out of the ground. China also found new oil sources but again it cost them about seventy dollars a barrel to get it out of the ground.

The Saudis needed seven or eight dollars a barrel. Their blue collar workers did not have the same labor union affiliations as our workers did. If oil prices stayed high, the Middle East would be out of the oil business. This is why the Saudis wanted to keep oil prices under fifty dollars. If oil prices stayed under the fifty dollar level, many of the new wells would have to be capped until such time as the price of oil went higher than the cost to bring it out of the ground. Until that time, the Middle East would remain a significant supplier of oil in the world.

Chapter 28

In September, I attended a real estate networking party in downtown Brooklyn. It was sponsored by a large savings bank headquartered in Brooklyn. The bank was hoping that some of the real estate professionals in attendance would send mortgage business to them. The bank was very involved in the residential mortgage arena and also looking to expand their commercial mortgage portfolio.

About one hundred real estate agents were in attendance with many of the bank's senior real estate officers on hand. The president of the bank was present and mingling with the crowd. I had a chance to speak with him, and somehow our conversation turned to the economy.

I mentioned that I was trying to save the economy by bringing down Morgan for manipulating the oil prices along with many other commodities and that a number of other banks were participating in the free for all.

"You should stick to real estate. That's your area. Don't get involved in other matters," he advised me with a stern look on his face.

"Is your bank involved with this manipulation?" I queried with a slight smirk on my face.

"Just stick to the real estate," he responded before walking off. Maybe I hit a nerve. I think I did. He had on a very nice suit with a subdued plaid pattern, well attired for a bank president. I wonder how he would look in prison stripes. I should have asked him.

As Election Day approached, I received a letter from my local state senator. He reminded me of all the wonderful things he has done for me during the last two years and foretold of the upcoming wonders if I voted for him again. If I needed anything just call the office.

He was the Senate Majority Leader. That sounds like an influential position. Maybe he could get some information from the AG's office. I dialed his number and was referred to an aide. She sounded bright and apparently somewhat senior in the office. I briefly explained what was going on and that the AG's office probably would not give her any specifics but all I really wanted to know was if something was going forward or if it was quashed again.

A few days later she got back to me. She said that I was right about them not giving up any specifics but that something was still going forward. Hallelujah!

Chapter 29

My dispatcher, Tommy, gave me a call taking two businesswomen from Lynbrook to midtown Manhattan. It was late afternoon, and the traffic going into Manhattan would be easy but coming out would be in rush hour. The return trip would be at least two hours.

The women were very pleasant and, as usual, I turned the conversation towards Morgan and my adventures in that regard.

"Aren't you worried about them trying to hurt you?" one asked.

"Not really, though, I have thought of it. But at some point don't you have to stand up for what is right?" I replied.

"But what if they try to kill you? They might try to shoot you while you are driving." She and her friend started to get very nervous, squirming in their seats and looking out the rear window. Every time a car came along side of us, I thought they would scream.

I couldn't resist having some fun with the situation. Although, I have been asked that question by a number of people and it may have some merit. I try not to think about it.

Looking in the rear view mirror, I said "That blue car has been behind us for quite a while. Do you think he may be tailing us?"

The women almost panicked. They were very relieved when I got them to their destination.

Chapter 30

One of my favorite dance partners is Bennye, short for Benita. She is a petite brunette with a poodle hair style. She is also very happily married for a long time to Al but Al doesn't dance. For me, dancing with Bennye is a good news bad news situation. The good news is that she dances with me because we dance well together, and I have known her a long time. I know that she is married. I don't hit on her and she feels safe. The bad news is that we dance well together. I have known her a long time. I know that she is married. I don't hit on her and she feels safe.

Bennye and Al hold a holiday party every December in their apartment. The apartment is small but cozy and for at least one evening a year it is wall-to-wall family and friends. A number of us usually seek shelter in a den where I have had some interesting conversations over the last few years. A year or two ago someone said "Why don't you write a book?" I have thought about that a lot since the party. I am not really a writer and never attempted anything like that before, but the idea sounded interesting.

Rocco, my closest friend at the limo service, has a Ph.D. in English Lit. There aren't too many educated people working in that business, so we have become close friends. The fact that we are both Viet Nam veterans has helped us bond even further. He hates teaching hence the limo job while he writes the great American novel.

Why would anybody opt out of working for a university twenty five hours a week, forty weeks per year, making two hundred thousand a year plus benefits when he could work seventy hours a week, fifty two weeks per year and make forty thousand a year with no benefits?

Rocco is somewhat verbose and emotional when he speaks. I often tease him that he could not order a hamburger at McDonald's in a thousand words or less and we laugh about it. On the other hand, if I wrote a book, it would be this is what happened, he did it, the end. It would probably be no more than six pages.

In college I probably wrote something that was five or six pages. Since then I have never written anything longer than a two page business letter. The thought of writing a book was interesting but absolutely terrifying to me.

My cousin Andrew in California is a very experienced movie producer and screenwriter. Upon my bringing up the subject of a book on my last visit, he gave me some good advice. "Just get started. By the time you get to the end, you will be a writer. Then you go back and redo the beginning." It took me many months of thinking about it before I struck the first letter on the keypad. I created a file on my computer and put a title on a new word document. I had officially started my book. It took many more weeks before I actually wrote a paragraph.

The fantasy of being an author and possibly getting a movie deal brings a smile to my face between sessions of knocking my head against the wall. Now when something frustrates me, I say "another chapter in the book," and then I hit my head against the wall.

The New York AG's office has been working on this for at least a year and a half to my knowledge. I have not heard any announcements of it charging anybody yet. It took the CFTC several months to do their investigation. I wonder what could be taking the AG's office so long. Everybody that I talk to who has any working knowledge of the office says that nothing meaningful will ever come out of this. The workings of the office are just too slipshod and inept. I pray that that is not the case.

Chapter 31

As I mentioned earlier, when cold calling people for sales I keep a record of what company, when I called and the person that I spoke to. I then call them again a year or two later. Maybe the situation has changed in their office and now they would be interested in my products. Very often the person that I spoke to who was not interested in my products may no longer be there and his replacement might be interested. You always keep trying.

Using this theory, I recently tried the Department of Justice again. I called the main number and a pleasant sounding receptionist answered. I asked who I should speak to regarding a possibly corrupt federal commissioner.

"Oh, let me put you right through to the Criminal Division." She connected me very promptly.

The woman who answered the phone at the Criminal Division seemed very nice and referred me to the Fraud

Unit. The Fraud Unit said that it was not in their area and that I had to speak with the FBI. She then forwarded me to the FBI. They just transfer you over and within seconds you are reconnected.

Very curtly, the FBI said I had to talk to the DOJ. I said that DOJ just transferred me to you. "You have to speak to the Inspector General's Division," and forwarded me before I could complain. The IG's office said that it wasn't in their purview and that I should talk to the Criminal Division.

"Wait a minute!" I screamed. "I just started with the Criminal Division five minutes ago, and I've been around the world three times. I have been passed around like a hot potato. The FBI sent me to you."

"Sorry sir. I would like to help you, but we don't handle that issue. That is their department." I can't make this stuff up. I am just not that clever. He transferred me back to the CD. The same voice answered. I told the nice lady at CD that I was just there on the phone and was passed around. She said that she did not know who I had talked with previously, but it wasn't her. It sure sounded a lot like her. She said that I should send an email to the CD office about my claim. Maybe one of the attorneys would look at it and call me back.

"Maybe?! What's maybe? What does maybe have to do with it?"

I informed her that this was in regard to the largest economic crime in the world, abetting terrorism and a possibly corrupt federal commissioner heading the oversight commission. What is maybe?

"Well, they are very busy."

"Very busy with what? Are they playing pinochle? Am I interrupting a card game? Is there something more important going on in the office?"

She said "Just send in an email." I sent an email that evening. I wrote down the exact sequence of whom I talked to so that I would remember it when I write my book. Then I went looking for a hard wall. Is my head getting a little flat on one side?

I called back several days later to make sure the CD had my email. They informed me that it had been received and someone would get back to me. That was in May just before Memorial Day. Did anyone get back to you? Nobody called me. I thought of calling the telephone company to see if my incoming calls were being blocked for some reason, but other people were getting through.

Just imagine if this was about something serious.

I called again after Labor Day looking to talk to someone in regard to my email. I finally got to talk to someone who did not sound like a receptionist. I think he was an attorney. (Was I making progress?) The gentleman sounded knowledgeable and I asked his name. "Sorry but it is official policy not to give our names." I can understand that. I asked about my email and he said that no one would act on it because I did not offer any proof. "That's why the FBI never responded to you. You did not offer any proof."

He knew about my calls to the FBI. They must have a file on me. I find this very interesting. Do they think of me as a crackpot or do they consider me a concerned citizen? I guess I will never know.

I could not believe what I was hearing. Is every citizen supposed to know what format to use when submitting information about major crimes to the FBI? Why didn't the duty officer that I was speaking with ask me if I had any proof to offer? I have had at least three conversations with the FBI in 2011 and also corresponded with them earlier when they saw my video. The word "proof" was never mentioned.

The first time I called the FBI in 2011 I must have spent fifteen or twenty minutes on the phone with the duty officer. Why didn't he ask for proof? The subsequent times I called the calls were shorter. Nobody wanted to talk to me because the previous guy didn't want to talk to me. Now DOJ doesn't want to talk to me because the FBI didn't want to talk to me. Absolutely amazing. If I hadn't actually been experiencing this, I would not believe it.

"How am I supposed to know what format to use? Why didn't you call me and ask for proof?"

"We don't have time for that. We are very busy."

"I can give you the names and phone numbers of my contacts at Commodity Futures and at Morgan Stanley. I believe that they will cooperate."

"We don't do that. You have to provide us with written and signed statements from them."

"I have to get the statements?! They won't give that to me. Who am I? But they would give it to you. I don't have a badge. You have the entire FBI." The volume started to go up.

"We don't do that. If we did that for you, we would have to do that for everybody and we do not have the time." I was starting to get a little heated.

"This is the most important economic event going on in the world, funding terrorism and bankrupting countries.

Fifteen million American families lost their homes and you can't make a phone call!? It's a local call. Commodity Futures is down the street from you!"

"We don't do that!"

"What do you mean that you don't do that? One phone call and you could save the world, but you don't do that."

"We are much too busy. We don't do that."

"You don't do that?! What the hell do you do?!" I hung up. I wonder what he put in my file after our conversation.

I really hope that he lost his shirt in the pinochle game.

Most people believe that their government never notices them, but now I know that I have my own personal file. How exciting! Does it say that I am a nice sincere guy trying to save the world or just another jackass crackpot harassing poor government employees? I guess I will never know except maybe if I run for President or something of that nature. That is something I have no plans to do yet.

If anybody wants his own personal file, I might be able to give advice on how to get one. Maybe it can be a new consulting business for me.

If I had not experienced it myself, I would not believe what had just gone on. Three conversations with the FBI and the word proof was not ever mentioned. The FBI decides not to respond to me because they never asked about proof. Then the DOJ looks at the FBI file and decides not to respond because the FBI did not respond and the biggest economic crime in our history continues to roll on.

Can you imagine if the FBI had asked me in our first conversation "Can you offer us any proof?" How different things may have been? Imagine if the worldwide recession ended four years earlier. It absolutely boggles my mind.

Maybe the DOJ should consider an advertising campaign to inform the public on how to submit information to the FBI. Just in case you ever come across a terrorist plot to blow up a city, it would be very handy to have taken a course so that you know the proper way to call it in.

It is possible that they thought of advertising in this manner, but their budget may have been cut because of the recession.

It is important to look at what might happen if the government did act in the manner that I am asking them to. Just imagine the FBI taking the CEO of Morgan out of his office in hand cuffs. On his way out, he tells his assistant to have the tankers tie up at the dock until he says otherwise. Morgan owns the Heidmar line, probably in an offshore corporation, with over six hundred tankers, about one third of all the oil tankers in the world. What would happen if they suddenly stopped? Could the U.S. Government seize some of the tankers to keep oil flowing into the ports or is Morgan just too big to be stopped? Could our Navy or Coast Guard operate these vessels on an interim basis? How long could some ports go without oil?

I also do not believe in the "too big to fail" concept. If an investment bank such as Morgan or Goldman were forced to shut down because of its commodity traders, I believe that many of the fragmented entities would survive under new names.

For example, the stock traders would move across the street with their same client lists in hand and continue to function under a new name. The real estate group would take office space around the corner and become MS Realty Advisors doing the same business with the same clients and contacts file they were working with previously. The bond traders and the wealth management group would make similar moves or be absorbed into other companies.

The world will simply not collapse because one of these companies went under. Just imagine if a Chief Executive Officer from one of these banks went to jail for twenty years. Do you think that other CEOs would stop condoning illegal practices even if they were profitable and force their employees to play closer to the rules? I think so.

These are very important things to consider and plan for. I believe that we must go forward and bite the bullet if necessary. If we do not, we are telling Morgan and others that we are willing to lie down on the sacrificial pyre at their convenience. I, for one, will never accept that.

The ICE recently bought the New York Stock Exchange. Now you no longer have the foxes guarding the henhouse. They have taken over the whole farm and are ordering truckloads of charcoal and barbecue sauce.

It is time to start writing.

Epilogue

Shortly after overthrowing Mubarak, the Egyptians realized they had made a mistake as the Muslim Brotherhood was much harsher than the previous regime. The Brotherhood's strict fundamentalism was not what the Egyptians were looking for. Together with the military leaders of the former Mubarak regime, the populace overthrew the Muslim Brotherhood. Things have been relatively stable and peaceful in Egypt since.

With a weakened Muslim Brotherhood in Syria, the Islamic State (ISIS) took control of the revolution and has destabilized the region and become a significant terrorist threat throughout the world. ISIS believes in, or at least claims to, a harsher fundamentalist lifestyle than even the Muslim Brotherhood. ISIS also wants to kill anybody who does not believe the way they do.

In late summer 2014, the New York State Attorney General's office apparently approached Morgan Stanley, Goldman Sachs, and possibly other banks and said "STOP". Oil prices have dropped significantly. Morgan and Goldman are getting out of the oil business. It is my understanding that nobody went to jail, and no money was fined. I feel sorry for the insiders who were whistle blowers. They put their jobs and careers on the line and probably will see nothing for it.

At about the same time, Saudi Arabia said screw the Intercontinental Exchange (ICE) and announced that they were going to sell oil directly to their customers and not go through the ICE. They started selling oil at forty-five dollars a barrel. The Saudis had tried to get oil prices down on several occasions, but the ICE always countered them. The Saudis did not do it for concern of the world economy. They did it for self-preservation.

A great deal of new oil has been found throughout North America, China and Russia but it costs fifty to eighty dollars a barrel to get it out of the ground. If oil prices stayed high, the Saudi oil would not be needed and they would have to find another source of income. The concept of finding a new source of revenue to maintain their lifestyle did not sit favorably with them. The Saudis are currently planning for a future existence after oil.

I expect that in the next few years, the North American oil companies will find more efficient methods of extracting their oil and that will bring their costs down. I hope that much of the new oil will find its way to the market.

During the recent period of inflated oil prices, worldwide demand for oil dropped by approximately twenty percent as every user tried to find more efficient methods to use energy. Every windmill, every solar panel, every hybrid automobile, and every conversion to natural gas has helped reduce the global demand for oil. Between this and the fact that sanctions against Iranian oil have been lifted, there is a significant glut on the world market. Prices dropped to the mid twenty dollar range.

The precipitous drop in oil prices caused some chaos in the American and Canadian oil patches. China was jolted which resulted in significant ripple effects on the global stock markets.

With the drop in oil prices, the United States economy started to pick up on day one. People were going back to restaurants. The retail sector saw increased sales almost immediately, demand for employees increased and salaries started up. Cautious spending by governments increased as city, county, and state sales tax revenues increased and their expenses went down.

It is my understanding that economies around the world have rebounded significantly.

The New Jersey county that had so much trouble trying to test my products is now a customer. I returned to the real estate business. Between the lubricants and the real estate, I no longer drive a limo.

Construction has picked up in almost all sectors and demand for lobsters has increased. During the recession, the lobstermen were getting $3.50–4.00 per pound for the best quality lobsters. Now they are getting $5.50–6.75 and their fuel costs have been cut in half.

Russia and Saudi Arabia came to an understanding and agreed to reduce their respective oil outputs. Oil prices started back up to the high thirty dollar range. I believe that oil prices will stabilize around the forty-five to fifty dollar level and swing in a range of five dollars up or down from that point. I believe that this price level will be around for some time.

The state senator who reminded me of all the wonderful things he did for me and foretold of the great things to come if I voted for him again was recently found guilty of eight counts of bribery, extortion, and conspiracy. Power corrupts and he was very powerful. He probably will never see daylight again. I hope his aide, who I thought was so competent, finds new employment.

The American national distributor of my products and the Canadian parent company took big hits initially as they lost sales to their respective oil patches, but almost as quickly, sales to local governments, who could not buy previously, compensated for them.

In September, 2016, the Federal Open Market Committee, FOMC, voted not to raise interest rates at that time. The FOMC is charged with setting United States monetary policy. If the economy is too sluggish, it lowers rates to spur business activity and cash flow. If the economy is overheated and inflation too high, the FOMC will raise rates to slow things down and keep the economic growth within the targeted range.

The day after the FOMC vote, Janet Yellin, Chairwoman of the FOMC, explained the reasons the Commission had for not raising rates. After citing many pertinent statistics and stating that the economy was moving in the right direction, she said that it was household spending that was driving the economy. I looked back at my television with a smile on my face and said "You're welcome."

On January 20th, 2017, Donald J. Trump was inaugurated as President of the United States. He quickly appointed six Goldman Sachs people to key positions. Will they police their friends or run the country for the benefit of their friends? Will they allow their friends to manipulate global markets to the detriment of all others? Only time will tell.

Thank you to all the whistleblowers, those who did not suffer from "Wall Street reporter's syndrome" and were willing to put their butts on the line to do the right thing. You will always be welcome here at the asylum.

Having even one finger in helping save the world economy is a wonderful feeling. You should try it some time.

Contact Information

For comments, speaking engagements and special orders contact author at mkhoffman@optonline.net

Please Review!

All independent authors depend upon reviews left on Amazon.com by readers to help promote their books. Without these reviews, they will hardly get any notice. Please take the time to leave a short review. Simply go to Amazon.com, find the book and go to the book's page. Under the author's name will be a list of reviews and stars. Click here and there will be a big button saying "Create your own review".

IT ONLY TAKES A MINUTE!

www.ingramcontent.com/pod-product-compliance
Lightning Source LLC
Chambersburg PA
CBHW070102080526
44586CB00013B/1158